REVISE EDEXCEL GCSE (9–1)
Chemistry
Foundation

REVISION WORKBOOK

Series Consultant: Harry Smith
Author: Nigel Saunders

A note from the publisher

In order to ensure that this resource offers high-quality support for the associated Pearson qualification, it has been through a review process by the awarding body. This process confirms that this resource fully covers the teaching and learning content of the specification or part of a specification at which it is aimed. It also confirms that it demonstrates an appropriate balance between the development of subject skills, knowledge and understanding, in addition to preparation for assessment.

Endorsement does not cover any guidance on assessment activities or processes (e.g. practice questions or advice on how to answer assessment questions), included in the resource nor does it prescribe any particular approach to the teaching or delivery of a related course.

While the publishers have made every attempt to ensure that advice on the qualification and its assessment is accurate, the official specification and associated assessment guidance materials are the only authoritative source of information and should always be referred to for definitive guidance.

Pearson examiners have not contributed to any sections in this resource relevant to examination papers for which they have responsibility.

Examiners will not use endorsed resources as a source of material for any assessment set by Pearson.

Endorsement of a resource does not mean that the resource is required to achieve this Pearson qualification, nor does it mean that it is the only suitable material available to support the qualification, and any resource lists produced by the awarding body shall include this and other appropriate resources.

Question difficulty

Look at this scale next to each exam-style question. It tells you how difficult the question is.

For the full range of Pearson revision titles across KS2, KS3, GCSE, Functional Skills, AS/A Level and BTEC visit:
www.pearsonschools.co.uk/revise

Contents

- - - - - - - - - - - - - - -

A small bit of small print: Edexcel
publishes Sample Assessment Material
and the Specification on its website.
This is the official content and this book
should be used in conjunction with it.
The questions have been written to help
you practise every topic in the book.
Remember: the real exam questions may
not look like this.

Formulae

1 Which of the following is the formula for calcium carbonate?

    ☐ **A** $CaCO$

    ☐ **B** $CaCO_2$

    ☐ **C** $CaCO_3$

    ☐ **D** $CaCO_4$ **(1 mark)**

> Put a cross in **one** box. Always answer multiple-choice questions, even if you don't actually know the answer.

2 Chlorine is used to kill harmful microorganisms in drinking water. Its formula is Cl_2. Place a tick (✓) in each correct box to describe what this formula tells you.

Cl_2 tells you that:	Tick (✓)
chlorine is an element	
chlorine is a compound	
chlorine is a mixture of atoms	
chlorine exists as molecules	

         (2 marks)

3 Complete the table to show the formulae of some common substances.

Substance	water	carbon dioxide	methane	sulfuric acid	sodium
Formula					

         (5 marks)

4 State what is meant by the term '**element**'.

> **Guided**

An element is a substance made from...

with the same number of.. **(2 marks)**

5 The formula for aluminium hydroxide is $Al(OH)_3$.

    (a) Deduce the number of elements in the formula $Al(OH)_3$.

.... **(1 mark)**

    (b) Deduce the total number of atoms in the formula $Al(OH)_3$.

.... **(1 mark)**

6 The formula for a carbonate ion is CO_3^{2-}.

    (a) State how you can tell that this is the formula for an ion.

.... **(1 mark)**

    (b) Describe what the numbers in the formula tell you about a carbonate ion.

....

.... **(2 marks)**

Equations

 1 Which of these statements describes a chemical reaction?

☐ **A** Reactants form from products.

☐ **B** Products form from reactants.

☐ **C** An element changes into another element.

> Answer C cannot be correct because one element cannot change to another element in chemical reactions.

☐ **D** The total mass of substances goes down.

(1 mark)

 2 The word equation for the thermal decomposition of copper carbonate is:

copper carbonate → copper oxide + carbon dioxide

Complete the table by placing a tick (✓) in one box in each row to show if a substance is a product or a reactant in this reaction.

Substance	Reactant	Product
copper oxide		
copper carbonate		
carbon dioxide		

(2 marks)

 3 Sodium hydroxide solution reacts with dilute hydrochloric acid to form sodium chloride and water.

Write the word equation for this reaction.

.... **(1 mark)**

 4 A teacher adds a piece of sodium metal to some water. The reaction produces sodium hydroxide solution and bubbles of hydrogen. Complete the balanced equation below to show the correct state symbols.

> You should be able to use the state symbols (s), (l), (g) and (aq).

Guided

$2Na(........) + 2H_2O(........) \rightarrow 2NaOH(........) + H_2(........)$ .... **(1 mark)**

 5 Balance the following equations by adding balancing numbers in the space provided.

> Do not add state symbols unless you are asked for them.

 Guided   (a) $2Cu + O_2 \rightarrow .....CuO$ **(1 mark)**

(b) $.....Al + Fe_2O_3 \rightarrow Al_2O_3 + ...Fe$ **(1 mark)**

(c) $Mg + ...HNO_3 \rightarrow Mg(NO_3)_2 + H_2$ **(1 mark)**

(d) $Na_2CO_3 + ...HCl \rightarrow .....NaCl + H_2O + CO_2$ **(1 mark)**

(e) $Cl_2 + ...NaBr \rightarrow .....NaCl + Br_2$ **(1 mark)**

(f) $.....Fe + ...O_2 \rightarrow .....Fe_2O_3$ **(1 mark)**

Hazards, risks and precautions

1 Complete the diagram below using a straight line to connect each hazard symbol to its correct description.

> **Guided**

| Symbol | Description |

flammable

may easily catch fire

oxidising agent

may cause other substances to catch fire, or make a fire worse

corrosive

causes severe damage to skin and eyes

harmful or irritant

health hazard

toxic

may cause death by inhalation, ingestion or skin contact

(4 marks)

2 Hazard symbols are found on containers. Give **two** reasons why these hazard symbols are used.

1 ....

2 .... **(2 marks)**

3 Describe what is meant by the term '**hazard**'.

> **Guided**

A hazard is something that could cause ....

or cause .... **(2 marks)**

4 Describe what is meant by the term '**risk**'.

> **Guided**

Risk is the chance that ....

> Risk and hazard are **not** the same thing.

....

.... **(2 marks)**

5 Copper reacts with concentrated nitric acid. The reaction forms copper nitrate, water and nitrogen dioxide. Nitrogen dioxide is a toxic brown gas with an irritating odour.

(a) Give **one** suitable precaution, other than eye protection, needed for safe working in this experiment.

.... **(1 mark)**

(b) Give a reason that explains your answer to part (**a**).

.... **(1 mark)**

3

Atomic structure

1 How much smaller is the nucleus of an atom compared with the overall size of the atom?

☐ **A** about 10 times smaller

☐ **B** about 100 times smaller

☐ **C** about 1000 times smaller

☐ **D** about 100 000 times smaller   **(1 mark)**

2 Which of these statements correctly describes an atom?

☐ **A** Most of the mass is concentrated in the nucleus.

☐ **B** Most of the charge is concentrated in the nucleus.

☐ **C** The number of neutrons always equals the number of protons.

☐ **D** The number of electrons always equals the number of neutrons.   **(1 mark)**

3 Atoms contain protons, neutrons and electrons. Place a tick (✓) in each correct box to show where these particles are found in atoms.

	Protons	Neutrons	Electrons
Nucleus			
Shells			

(2 marks)

4 Complete the table to show the relative mass and relative charge of each particle in an atom.

> **Guided**

Particle	Proton	Neutron	Electron
Relative mass		1	
Relative charge			−1

(2 marks)

5 Atoms contain equal numbers of protons and electrons. For example, a hydrogen atom contains one proton and one electron.

> Think about the charges carried by protons and electrons.

Explain why the overall charge of an atom is zero.

....

.... **(2 marks)**

6 John Dalton described his model of the atom in 1803.

Suggest a reason to explain why his model did not include protons, neutrons and electrons.

.... **(1 mark)**

Isotopes

1 State what is meant by the **mass number** of an atom.

> **Guided**

The mass number of an atom is the total number of ....

.... **(1 mark)**

2 An atom of an element X has an atomic number 9 and a mass number 19. How many electrons does an atom of element X contain?

   ☐ **A** 9

   ☐ **B** 10

   ☐ **C** 19

   ☐ **D** 28

(1 mark)

3 Describe, in terms of the particles in its atoms, what an element is.

> **Guided**

An element consists of atoms that have the same number of ....

in the nucleus, and this is different for different .... **(2 marks)**

4 Three isotopes of hydrogen are ^1_1H (hydrogen-1), ^2_1H (hydrogen-2) and ^3_1H (hydrogen-3).

> **Guided**

   (a) Complete the table to show the numbers of protons, neutrons and electrons in an atom of each isotope.

Isotope	Protons	Neutrons	Electrons
hydrogen-1	1		1
hydrogen-2		1	
hydrogen-3			

(3 marks)

   (b) Explain, in terms of the particles in the atom, why these are isotopes of the same element.

Isotopes of an element have atoms with the same number of ....

but different numbers of .... **(2 marks)**

5 Chlorine has a relative atomic mass of 35.5 but some elements have relative atomic masses that are whole numbers. Explain why the relative atomic masses of some elements are *not* whole numbers.

> Think about whether all the atoms of an element are the same.

....

....

.... **(2 marks)**

Mendeleev's table

1 (a) How did Mendeleev **first** arrange the elements in his periodic table?

☐ **A** in the order of increasing number of protons in the nucleus

☐ **B** in the order of increasing reactivity with other elements

☐ **C** in the order of increasing number of isotopes

☐ **D** in the order of increasing relative atomic mass   **(1 mark)**

(b) State **one** factor, other than the one in your answer to part (**a**), that Mendeleev used when he arranged the elements.

> What are the similarities and differences between elements?

.... **(1 mark)**

2 The diagram shows part of Mendeleev's 1871 table.

			Group			
1	2	3	4	5	6	7
H						
Li	Be	B	C	N	O	F
Na	Mg	Al	Si	P	S	Cl
K Cu	Ca Zn	* *	Ti *	V As	Cr Se	Mn Br
Rb Ag	Sr Cd	Y In	Zr Sn	Nb Sb	Mo Te	* I

(a) Give **one** similarity between this table and the modern periodic table.

> Remember that you will be given a periodic table in the exam. There is also one at the back of this book.

.... **(1 mark)**

(b) The * symbols in the diagram above represent gaps that Mendeleev left in his table.

  (i) Give **two** other differences between this table and the modern periodic table.

    1: ....

    2: .... **(2 marks)**

  (ii) Describe one useful thing that Mendeleev was able to do using information about the elements next to the gaps in his table.

    ....

    .... **(1 mark)**

3 Mendeleev had difficulty placing some elements. For example, the order of tellurium $^{128}_{53}$Te and iodine $^{127}_{54}$I appeared to be reversed in his table. Explain, in terms of atomic structure, why the positions of these two elements were actually correct.

Tellurium has a .... relative atomic mass than iodine does.

However, iodine atoms have .... protons than tellurium atoms.   **(2 marks)**

The periodic table

1 How are the elements arranged in the modern periodic table?

☐ **A** in order of increasing mass number

☐ **B** in order of increasing atomic number

☐ **C** in order of increasing nucleon number

☐ **D** in order of increasing numbers of electron shells   **(1 mark)**

2 The positions of five elements (**A**, **B**, **C**, **D** and **E**) are shown in the periodic table below. These letters are **not** the chemical symbols for these elements.

(a) State the name given to a vertical column in the periodic table.

.... **(1 mark)**

(b) Give the letters of **two** elements that have similar chemical properties to each other.

.... **(1 mark)**

(c) Give the letters of **all** the metal elements.

> There are more metallic elements in the periodic table than non-metallic elements.

.... **(1 mark)**

(d) Give the letters of **two** elements in the same period.

.... **(1 mark)**

3 The meaning of the term '**atomic number**' has changed over time because of the discovery of subatomic particles.

Guided

(a) Give the meaning of the term '**atomic number**' as Mendeleev might have understood it in the nineteenth century.

the position of ....

.... **(1 mark)**

(b) Give the modern meaning of the term '**atomic number**'.

the number of ....

in an atom's .... **(2 marks)**

Electronic configurations

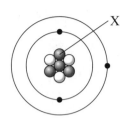

1 The diagram shows a lithium atom. It is not drawn to scale.

(a) State the electronic configuration of lithium.

> Count the number of electrons in each shell in the diagram.

.... **(1 mark)**

Guided

(b) Deduce the name of the shaded particle labelled **X**, and explain your answer.

There are three electrons, so there must be three ....

so the four shaded circles must be .... **(2 marks)**

(c) Oxygen (atomic number 8) has eight electrons in its atoms.

> The first electron shell can hold only a maximum of two electrons.

Draw a diagram to show the arrangement of electrons in an oxygen atom.

> You need to show both electron shells and all eight electrons, but you can show the nucleus as a single dot.

(2 marks)

2 The table shows some information about two non-metal elements, fluorine and chlorine.

Guided

Non-metal	Atomic number	Electronic configuration
F	9	2.7
Cl	17	2.8.7

(a) Explain, in terms of electronic configurations, why fluorine and chlorine are placed in group 7.

Both have ....

in their .... **(2 marks)**

(b) Explain, in terms of electronic configurations, why fluorine and chlorine are **not** in the same period.

Fluorine has ....

but chlorine has .... **(2 marks)**

3 Deduce the electronic configurations of the following elements.

Guided

(a) phosphorus (atomic number 15)

    2.8... **(1 mark)**

(b) calcium (atomic number 20)

.... **(1 mark)**

4 State and explain the number of the group in which helium (electronic configuration 2) is placed.

....

.... **(2 marks)**

Ions

1 Which of the following statements correctly describes the formation of an ion?

> You can quickly narrow the alternatives if you know the correct name for each type of ion, or how it forms.

   ☐ **A** Positively charged ions, called cations, form when atoms or groups of atoms gain electrons.

   ☐ **B** Positively charged ions, called anions, form when atoms or groups of atoms lose electrons.

   ☐ **C** Negatively charged ions, called cations, form when atoms or groups of atoms lose electrons.

   ☐ **D** Negatively charged ions, called anions, form when atoms or groups of atoms gain electrons.

(1 mark)

Guided

2 The atomic number of magnesium, Mg, is 12. The symbol for a magnesium ion is Mg^{2+}.

   (a) Deduce the number of electrons in a magnesium **ion**.

     $12 - \ldots\ldots = $ .... **(1 mark)**

   (b) The electronic configuration for a calcium atom is 2.8.8.2. Write the electronic configuration of a calcium **ion**, Ca^{2+}.

   .... **(1 mark)**

Guided

3 Complete the table to show the numbers of protons, neutrons and electrons in each ion.

> 🖩 **Maths skills** Work out the number of electrons in an atom, then add or subtract electrons according to the charge shown.

Ion	Atomic number	Mass number	Protons	Neutrons	Electrons
N^{3-}	7	15	7	8	10
K^{+}	19	40			
Ca^{2+}	20	40			
S^{2-}	16	32			
Br^{-}	35	81			

(4 marks)

4 The diagram shows the formation of a sodium ion, Na^{+}, from a sodium atom.

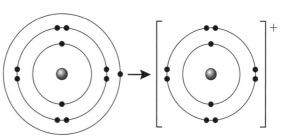

Draw a similar diagram to show the formation of a chloride ion, Cl^{-}, from a chlorine atom.

> Your diagram should look similar to the one above. However, the electronic configuration of a chlorine atom is 2.8.7 and a chloride ion forms when a chlorine atom gains one electron.

(3 marks)

Formulae of ionic compounds

1 The formula of a sodium ion is Na^+. The formula of a phosphate ion is PO_4^{3-}. Which of the following is the formula for sodium phosphate?

> Answer A cannot be correct because the sodium ion has fewer charges than the phosphate ion.

☐ **A** $NaPO_4$ ☐ **B** $Na(PO_4)_3$ ☐ **C** Na_2PO_4 ☐ **D** Na_3PO_4 **(1 mark)**

2 Complete the table to show the formulae of the compounds produced by each pair of ions.

> You need to know the formulae of common ions. This helps you work out the formulae of ionic substances.

> **Maths skills** An ionic compound contains equal numbers of positive and negative *charges*, but not always equal numbers of positive and negative *ions*. Look at the completed examples to help you.

Guided

	Cl^-	S^{2-}	OH^-	NO_3^-	SO_4^{2-}
K^+				KNO_3	
Ca^{2+}			$Ca(OH)_2$		$CaSO_4$
Fe^{3+}		Fe_2S_3			
NH_4^+	NH_4Cl				

(15 marks)

3 Magnesium ribbon burns in air. It reacts with oxygen to produce magnesium oxide.

(a) Balance this equation for the reaction.

……$Mg + O_2 \rightarrow$ ……MgO **(1 mark)**

(b) Magnesium nitride is also formed, as some of the hot magnesium reacts with nitrogen in the air.

> Think about how many electrons a nitrogen atom must lose or gain to obtain a full outer shell.

(i) Nitrogen is in group 5. Suggest reasons that explain why the formula for a nitride ion is N^{3-}.

....

.... **(2 marks)**

(ii) Write the formula for magnesium nitride.

> The formula for a magnesium ion is Mg^{2+}.

.... **(1 mark)**

(iii) Explain why the NO_3^- ion is called the nitrate ion, but the N^{3-} ion is called the nitride ion.

....

.... **(2 marks)**

4 Complete the table to show the names of the ions.

> Remember to use the endings -ide and -ate correctly. Look again at question 3 (b) (iii) to help you.

	S^{2-}	SO_4^{2-}	Cl^-	ClO_3^-
Name				

(4 marks)

> S is the chemical symbol for sulfur and Cl is the chemical symbol for chlorine.

Properties of ionic compounds

1 Which statement about the formation of ionic compounds, such as sodium chloride, is correct?

☐ **A** Electrons are transferred from metal atoms to non-metal atoms, producing cations and anions.

☐ **B** Electrons are transferred from cations to anions, producing metal atoms and non-metal atoms.

☐ **C** Electrons are shared between metal atoms and non-metal atoms.

☐ **D** Electrons are shared between cations and anions. **(1 mark)**

2 Ionic compounds have a lattice structure.

(a) Complete the diagram, using the symbols + and –, to show the positions of positive and negative ions in an ionic lattice.

> **Maths skills** Remember that opposite charges will attract each other and like charges will repel.

> You should be able to visualise and represent 2D and 3D forms, including 2D models of 3D objects. **(1 mark)**

> Guided

(b) Describe what ionic bonds are.

There are strong ....

between .... **(2 marks)**

3 Explain why ionic compounds have high melting points and boiling points.

> Bonds between the particles in an ionic substance must be broken during melting and boiling. Think about whether this involves a relatively low or high amount of energy, and why.

....

.... **(2 marks)**

4 Ionic compounds such as sodium chloride can conduct electricity in some situations.

(a) Complete the table by placing a tick (✓) in each **correct** box to show where ionic compounds conduct electricity.

> You do not need to tick all the boxes.

Ionic compound is:	solid	liquid	dissolved in water
conducts electricity			

(1 mark)

(b) State what the ions in an ionic compound must be able to do for it to conduct electricity.

.... **(1 mark)**

Covalent bonds

1 What are the typical sizes of atoms and small molecules?

> **Maths skills** The quantities are shown in standard form. For example, 10^{-3} is greater than 10^{-6}.

	Atoms	Molecules
☐ A	10^{-10} m	10^{-11} m
☐ B	10^{-9} m	10^{-12} m
☐ C	10^{-10} m	10^{-9} m
☐ D	10^{-12} m	10^{-9} m

> Answer A cannot be correct because it shows atoms as being larger than small molecules.

(1 mark)

2 Explain how a covalent bond forms.

> How many electrons are involved in a covalent bond?

Guided

A covalent bond forms when ....

between .... **(2 marks)**

3 Hydrogen reacts with fluorine to form hydrogen fluoride: $H_2 + F_2 \rightarrow 2HF$

The electronic configuration of hydrogen is 1 and the electronic configuration of fluorine is 2.7.

(a) Describe what the structure, H–F, tells you about a hydrogen fluoride molecule.

....

.... **(2 marks)**

(b) A dot-and-cross diagram for a molecule of fluorine, F_2, is shown below.

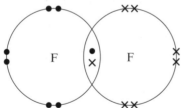

> Show each chemical symbol. Show one atom's electrons as dots and the other atom's electrons as crosses.

Draw a dot-and-cross diagram for a molecule of hydrogen fluoride, HF. Show the outer electrons only.

(2 marks)

4 Oxygen atoms have six electrons in their outer shell. Draw a dot-and-cross diagram for an oxygen molecule, O_2. Show the outer electrons only.

> The displayed formula for oxygen is O=O.

(2 marks)

Simple molecular substances

1 Carbon dioxide, CO_2, is found in the air.
   Why does it have a low boiling point?

   > Answer A cannot be correct
   > because covalent bonds are strong.

   ☐ **A** There are weak covalent bonds between carbon atoms and oxygen atoms.

   ☐ **B** There are weak forces of attraction between carbon atoms and oxygen atoms.

   ☐ **C** There are weak forces of attraction between carbon dioxide molecules.

   ☐ **D** There are weak covalent bonds between carbon dioxide molecules.   **(1 mark)**

2 The table shows the properties of four different substances (**A**, **B**, **C** and **D**).

Substance	Melting point (°C)	Conducts electricity when solid?	Conducts electricity when liquid?	Solubility in water (g per 100 g of water)
A	290	no	yes	43
B	−39	yes	yes	0
C	−95	no	no	0.001
D	660	yes	yes	0

   (a) State which substance (**A**, **B**, **C** or **D**) is a simple molecular substance.

   .... **(1 mark)**

   (b) Explain your answer to part (**a**).

   > Which of the properties of your chosen substance
   > are typical of simple molecular substances?

   ....

   .... **(2 marks)**

3 Sulfur hexafluoride, SF_6, exists as simple molecules. It is used as an insulating gas
   for electrical equipment.

   (a) Explain why sulfur hexafluoride does not conduct electricity.

   > Substances that conduct electricity have electrically charged particles that are free
   > to move around. Think about whether simple molecules are electrically charged or
   > contain electrons that are free to move.

   ....

   .... **(2 marks)**

> Guided

   (b) Suggest reasons to explain why sulfur hexafluoride does not dissolve in water.

   The intermolecular forces between ....

   ....

   are weaker than those between ....

   and those between .... **(3 marks)**

Giant molecular substances

1 Silica, SiO_2, does not dissolve in water. It does not conduct electricity, even when molten, and its melting point is very high.

> Answer D cannot be correct because metals, not molecules, contain metallic bonds.

Which statement describes a molecule of silica?

☐ **A** a giant molecule with ionic bonds ☐ **C** a simple molecule with covalent bonds

☐ **B** a giant molecule with covalent bonds ☐ **D** a simple molecule with metallic bonds

(1 mark)

2 The diagrams show the structures of diamond and graphite.

> You should be able to visualise and represent 2D and 3D forms, including 2D representations of 3D objects.

diamond   graphite

(a) Name the element with atoms that form both diamond and graphite.

.... **(1 mark)**

(b) State the maximum number of bonds present between each atom in a molecule of diamond.

> Count the bonds between the atoms in the diagram of diamond. What is the highest number you get?

.... **(1 mark)**

(c) Name the type of structure shown in both diagrams.

.... **(1 mark)**

3 Refer to structure and bonding in your answers to the following questions.

Guided

(a) Explain why graphite is suitable for use as a lubricant. | Lubricants must be slippery. |

The layers in graphite can ....

because .... **(2 marks)**

(b) Explain why graphite is used to make electrodes.

> You need to explain why graphite can conduct electricity, just as metals can.

Atoms in graphite can form only three ....

so graphite has .... **(2 marks)**

(c) Explain why diamond is suitable for use in cutting tools.

> You need to explain why diamond is very hard.

Diamond has a .... structure, and its atoms

....

are joined by many .... **(2 marks)**

Other large molecules

1 Ethene, C_2H_4, can be made into a polymer. What is the name of this polymer?

☐ **A** poly(ethanol)   ☐ **C** poly(ethene)

☐ **B** poly(ethane)   ☐ **D** poly(ethyne)   **(1 mark)**

2 The diagram is a model of a section of a simple polymer.

(a) Name the element with atoms represented by the larger, dark-grey balls in the diagram.

.... **(1 mark)**

(b) Name the type of bonding present in a molecule of this polymer.

.... **(1 mark)**

3 Fullerenes are forms of carbon that include hollow balls, such as buckminsterfullerene, C_{60}.

(a) Explain why buckminsterfullerene is a simple molecule, rather than a giant covalent substance.

....

....

.... **(2 marks)**

Guided

(b) Explain, in terms of its structure and bonding, why buckminsterfullerene has a much lower melting point than graphite.

> The strong covalent bonds between the carbon atoms in these molecules do *not* break during melting.

Buckminsterfullerene has a .... structure

so it has weak .... that are easily overcome. **(2 marks)**

4 Graphene is a form of carbon. It is a good conductor of electricity and has a very high melting point.

The diagram is a model of part of the structure of graphene.

Explain, in terms of its structure and bonding, why graphene has a very high melting point.

> Include the type of bonds that must be broken during melting.

....

....

.... **(3 marks)**

Metals

1   Which of the following correctly describes two typical properties of metals?

     ☐   **A**   shiny with high densities   ☐   **C**   dull with low densities

     ☐   **B**   shiny with low densities   ☐   **D**   dull with high densities   **(1 mark)**

2   Metal elements and non-metal elements have different typical properties.

    Complete the table below by placing a tick (✓) in each correct box.

	Low melting points	High melting points	Good conductors of electricity	Poor conductors of electricity
Metals				
Non-metals				

     (4 marks)

3   Metals are insoluble in water. Some metals react with water, forming soluble hydroxides and hydrogen. For example, a piece of sodium reacts with water to produce sodium hydroxide and hydrogen.

    (a)   State why fizzing is observed during this reaction.

     ....   **(1 mark)**

    (b)   Suggest reasons to explain why the piece of sodium seems to dissolve in water.

     ....

     ....   **(2 marks)**

4   Copper is a metal used in electricity cables. It is a good conductor of electricity and is malleable (it will bend without shattering). The diagram is a model for the structure of copper. Each circle is a copper ion.

    (a)   State two improvements to the diagram that will make it a more accurate model of the structure of copper.

> Remember that metal atoms form positively charged ions by losing electrons.

     (i)   ....

     (ii)   ....   **(2 marks)**

Guided

    (b)   Explain why copper is malleable.

     It has layers of ....

     which can ....   **(2 marks)**

    (c)   Explain why copper is a good conductor of electricity.

> A substance conducts electricity if it contains charged particles that are free to move around.

     ....

     ....   **(2 marks)**

Limitations of models

1 The formula of a substance can be given in different ways.

Which row (**A**, **B**, **C** or **D**) correctly shows the different formulae for ethene?

> Answer A cannot be correct because it describes ethane, not ethene.

	Molecular formula	Empirical formula	Structural formula
☐ **A**	C_2H_6	CH_3	CH_3CH_3
☐ **B**	C_2H_4	CH_2	$CH_2=CH_2$
☐ **C**	CH_2	C_2H_4	$CH_2=CH_2$
☐ **D**	$CH_2=CH_2$	C_2H_4	CH_2

(1 mark)

2 The diagrams (**A**, **B**, **C** and **D**) show four different models for a molecule of methane, CH_4.

A	B	C	D
H │ H—C—H │ H	(dot-and-cross diagram of methane)	(ball-and-stick model)	(space-filling model)
Structure	**Dot-and-cross diagram**	**Ball-and-stick model**	**Space-filling model**

State the letters (**A**, **B**, **C** or **D**) for all the models that:

> You may need to identify more than one model in your answers.

(a) show the covalent bonds present in a molecule .... **(1 mark)**

(b) identify the elements present in a molecule .... **(1 mark)**

(c) represent the three-dimensional shape of a molecule .... **(1 mark)**

(d) show the electrons involved in bonding.. **(1 mark)**

(e) show the relative sizes of each atom in a molecule. .... **(1 mark)**

Guided

3 A student wants to represent a water molecule. She decides to draw a dot-and-cross diagram rather than a ball-and-stick model because she finds this easier to do.

> Think about what a ball-and-stick model shows that a dot-and-cross diagram does not.

(a) Give one strength of a ball-and-stick model compared with a dot-and-cross diagram.

Unlike a dot-and-cross diagram, a ball-and-stick model ....

.... **(1 mark)**

(b) Other than the student's reason, give two weaknesses of a ball-and-stick model compared with a dot-and-cross diagram.

> Think about what a dot-and-cross model shows that a ball-and-stick model does not.

Unlike a dot-and-cross diagram, a ball-and-stick model does not show ....

....

or .... **(2 marks)**

Relative formula mass

Use the relative atomic masses, A_r, in the table below when you answer the questions.

Element	Al	Ca	Cl	Cu	H	N	O	S
A_r	27	40	35.5	63.5	1	14	16	32

> If relative atomic masses are not given in the question, you can find them in the periodic table.

1 Calculate the relative formula mass, M_r, of each of the following substances.

> You do not need to show your working out, but it will help you to check the accuracy of your answers.

 Guided

(a) chlorine, Cl_2

> You do not need to show a decimal point in your answer to this question.

$2 \times 35.5 = $ .... **(1 mark)**

Guided

(b) water, H_2O

$(2 \times 1) + 16 = 2 + 16 = $ .... **(1 mark)**

(c) sulfur dioxide, SO_2 .... **(1 mark)**

(d) aluminium oxide, Al_2O_3 .... **(1 mark)**

(e) ammonium chloride, NH_4Cl .... **(1 mark)**

> Do not round the answer to this question to a whole number.

(f) calcium chloride, $CaCl_2$ .... **(1 mark)**

(g) aluminium chloride, $AlCl_3$ .... **(1 mark)**

2 Calculate the relative formula mass, M_r, of each of the following substances.

(a) calcium hydroxide, $Ca(OH)_2$

Guided

$16 + 1 = 17, 17 \times 2 = 34, 40 + 34 = $ .... **(1 mark)**

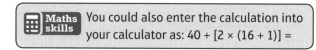 **Maths skills** You could also enter the calculation into your calculator as: $40 + [2 \times (16 + 1)] = $

(b) aluminium hydroxide, $Al(OH)_3$ .... **(1 mark)**

(c) calcium nitrate, $Ca(NO_3)_2$ .... **(1 mark)**

(d) ammonium sulfate, $(NH_4)_2SO_4$ .... **(1 mark)**

(e) aluminium sulfate, $Al_2(SO_4)_3$ .... **(1 mark)**

Practical skills **Empirical formulae**

1 A student carries out an experiment to determine the empirical formula of magnesium oxide. He heats a piece of magnesium ribbon in a crucible. He continues until the contents of the crucible stop glowing.

The table shows his results.

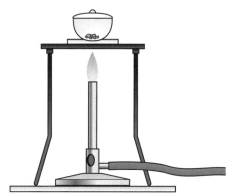

Object	Mass (g)
empty crucible and lid	20.25
crucible, lid and contents before heating	20.49
crucible, lid and contents after heating	20.65

(a) Suggest a reason to explain why:

(i) the student continued heating until the glowing stopped.

.... **(1 mark)**

(ii) the student briefly lifted the lid a few times during the experiment.

.... **(1 mark)**

(b) The hot crucible is a hazard. Explain one precaution to control the risk of harm from this hazard.

> Say what the student should do to avoid being harmed, and what harm this will prevent.

....

.... **(2 marks)**

2 Calculate the empirical formula of magnesium oxide using the student's results.

(A_r of Mg = 24 and A_r of O = 16)

mass of magnesium used = 20.49 g − 20.25 g = 0.24 g

mass of oxygen reacted = 20.65 g − 20.49 g = ...

$$\begin{array}{cc} \text{Mg} & \text{O} \\ \dfrac{0.24}{24} = 0.010 & \dfrac{........}{16} = ... \end{array}$$

> Divide the mass of each element by its A_r.

$$\dfrac{0.010}{........} = ... \qquad \dfrac{........}{........} = ...$$

> Divide both numbers by the smallest number to find the ratio.

Empirical formula is ....

> Write down the empirical formula. **(4 marks)**

3 The empirical formula of a sample of gas is NO_2. Its relative formula mass, M_r, is 92.

Deduce the molecular formula of the gas. (A_r of N = 14 and A_r of O = 16)

M_r of NO_2 = 14 + (2 × 16) = ...

factor needed = $\dfrac{92}{........}$ =

> **Maths skills** Calculate the M_r of NO_2. Then work out how many times this will go into 92. Multiply each number in the empirical formula by this factor to obtain the molecular formula.

Molecular formula is ....

(2 marks)

Conservation of mass

1 Sodium chloride solution reacts with silver nitrate solution. Sodium nitrate solution and a white precipitate of solid silver chloride form:

$NaCl(aq) + AgNO_3(aq) \rightarrow NaNO_3(aq) + AgCl(s)$

A student investigates the change in mass during this reaction. He sets up the apparatus shown in the diagram, then shakes the flask to mix the two solutions.

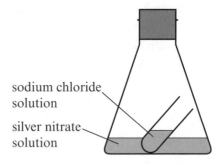

sodium chloride solution

silver nitrate solution

(a) State whether the reaction happens in a closed or a non-enclosed system. Give a reason for your answer.

type of system:...

reason:.. **(1 mark)**

(b) The student records the mass of the flask and its contents before and after the reaction.

(i) What happens to the mass during the reaction? <u>Underline</u> the correct answer.

It increases. | It decreases. | It stays the same.   **(1 mark)**

(ii) Give a reason for your answer to part (**i**).

.... **(1 mark)**

2 Copper carbonate decomposes, when heated, to form copper oxide and carbon dioxide:

$CuCO_3(s) \rightarrow CuO(s) + CO_2(g)$

> You do not need to calculate relative formula masses for this question.

8.2 g of copper carbonate formed 5.3 g of copper oxide.
Calculate the mass of carbon dioxide produced. Answer = ... **(1 mark)**

3 Sodium reacts with chlorine to form sodium chloride: $2Na(s) + Cl_2(g) \rightarrow 2NaCl(s)$

Calculate the maximum mass of sodium chloride that can be made from 142 g of chlorine.

(M_r of Cl_2 = 71 and M_r of NaCl = 58.5)

(1 × 71) = 71 g of Cl_2 makes (2 × 58.5) = 117 g of NaCl

142 g of Cl_2 makes 117 × (142/71) g of NaCl

= .... g   **(1 mark)**

4 Magnesium reacts with oxygen to form magnesium oxide: $2Mg(s) + O_2(g) \rightarrow 2MgO(s)$

Calculate the maximum mass of magnesium oxide that can be made from 12.6 g of oxygen.

> Remember to calculate the relative formula mass, M_r, of oxygen gas and magnesium oxide first.

(A_r of O = 16 and A_r of Mg = 24)

M_r of O_2 = ... M_r of MgO = ...

.... g of O_2 makes .... g of MgO

12.6 g of O_2 makes .... g of MgO

= .... g of MgO   **(3 marks)**

Concentration of solution

1 Sea water contains dissolved salts.

Which row (**A, B, C** or **D**) correctly describes the components of sea water?

☐ **A**
☐ **B**
☐ **C**
☐ **D**

	Solute	Solvent	Solution
A	water	salt	sea water
B	salt	sea water	water
C	sea water	salt	water
D	salt	water	sea water

(1 mark)

2 Calculate the following volumes in dm^3.

[Maths skills] $1\,dm^3 = 1000\,cm^3$.

> **Guided**

(a) $2500\,cm^3$

$$volume = \frac{2500}{1000} = \text{.............. } dm^3$$

(1 mark)

(b) $500\,cm^3$

.... **(1 mark)**

(c) $25\,cm^3$

.... **(1 mark)**

3 Calculate the concentrations of the following solutions in $g\,dm^{-3}$:

(a) $50\,g$ of sodium hydroxide dissolved in $2\,dm^3$ of water

.... **(1 mark)**

(b) $14.6\,g$ of hydrogen chloride dissolved in $0.400\,dm^3$ of water

.... **(1 mark)**

(c) $0.25\,g$ of glucose dissolved in $0.050\,dm^3$ of water.

.... **(1 mark)**

4 A student dissolves $10\,g$ of copper sulfate in $250\,cm^3$ of water. Calculate the concentration of the solution formed in $g\,dm^{-3}$.

> **Guided**

$$concentration = \left(\frac{10}{250}\right) \times 1000 = \text{......................................}$$ **(1 mark)**

5 A student dissolves $2.0\,g$ of silver nitrate in $125\,cm^3$ of water. Calculate the concentration of the solution formed in $g\,dm^{-3}$.

.... **(1 mark)**

6 A school technician wants to make $2.5\,dm^3$ of a $40\,g\,dm^{-3}$ aqueous solution of sodium hydroxide.

(a) Describe the meaning of the term '**aqueous solution**'.

.... **(1 mark)**

(b) Calculate the mass of sodium hydroxide that the technician must dissolve to make her solution.

[Maths skills] Rearrange this equation.

$$concentration\ in\ g\,dm^{-3} = \frac{mass\ of\ solute}{volume\ of\ solution\ in\ dm^3}$$

.... **(1 mark)**

Extended response – Types of substance

*Graphite and diamond are two different forms of carbon. The table shows some information about their properties. Copper, a soft metal used in electrical cables, is included for comparison.

Substance	Relative hardness	Relative electrical conductivity
graphite	10	10^8
copper	100	10^{10}
diamond	10 000	1

> Higher values mean harder or better at conducting electricity.

Graphite is used to make electrodes and as a lubricant. Diamond is used in cutting tools.

Describe, using information from the table, the properties of graphite and diamond that make them suitable for these uses. Explain these properties in terms of the bonding and structure present.

> You should be able to describe the structures of graphite and diamond.

> It may help if you plan your answer before you start. For example, write separate answers about graphite and diamond. Include each given use and, using information from the table, the property important to that use. Make sure that you then explain how the substance's bonding and structure give it that property.

....

....

....

....

....

....

....

....

....

....

....

....

.... **(6 marks)**

> Quick, labelled diagrams showing the structures of diamond and graphite may help your explanations.

States of matter

1 Iodine crystals become a purple vapour when they are warmed. What is the name for this state change?

> The crystals are in the solid state and the vapour is in the gas state.

☐ **A** melting   ☐ **B** boiling   ☐ **C** subliming   ☐ **D** condensing   **(1 mark)**

2 Most substances can exist in the solid, liquid or gas states. Give the name of each state change below.

(a) liquid to solid

.... **(1 mark)**

(b) gas to liquid

.... **(1 mark)**

3 Water changes to steam when it is heated. State why this is a **physical** change.

.... **(1 mark)**

4 Particles are arranged in different ways in each state of matter. Place a tick (✓) in each correct box below.

State of matter	Particles are:			
	close together	far apart	randomly arranged	regularly arranged
solid				
liquid				
gas				

(3 marks)

5 (a) Name the state in which the particles move the fastest.

.... **(1 mark)**

(b) Particles in all states have some stored energy. Name the state in which the particles have the least stored energy, and justify your answer.

....

.... **(2 marks)**

6 The melting point of substance **X** is −114 °C and its boiling point is 78 °C. Predict its state at −30 °C.

> −30 °C is above −114 °C and below 78 °C.

.... **(1 mark)**

7 Describe what happens to the arrangement, and movement, of particles when a substance changes from the liquid state to the solid state.

> Guided

The arrangement changes from ....

and the movement changes from ....

.... **(2 marks)**

Pure substances and mixtures

1 Substances can be pure or they can be mixtures. Which of the following is a mixture?

☐ **A** carbon

☐ **B** oxygen

☐ **C** carbon dioxide

☐ **D** carbon dioxide solution   **(1 mark)**

2 The label on a carton of orange juice describes the contents as 'pure'. Explain why the orange juice is a mixture, rather than a pure substance, in the scientific sense.

....

....

.... **(3 marks)**

3 (a) Explain, in terms of subatomic particles, why sodium, Na, and chlorine, Cl_2, are two different elements.

> Write your answer in terms of a named subatomic particle found in the nucleus of all atoms.

The atoms of an element all have the same ....

but atoms of Na and Cl_2 have different .... **(2 marks)**

(b) Explain why sodium chloride, NaCl, is defined as a compound.

> Think about how many elements a compound contains, and whether or how these are joined together.

....

.... **(2 marks)**

4 A student investigates three samples of water. She transfers $25 \, cm^3$ of each sample to weighed evaporating basins. She then heats the basins until all the water has evaporated, lets them cool and weighs them again. The table shows the student's results.

Water sample	Mass of basin before adding water (g)	Mass of basin after evaporating water (g)	Difference in mass (g)
A	73.20	73.05	0.15
B	72.85	72.61	
C	74.43	74.40	

(a) Complete the table to show the difference in mass for water samples **B** and **C**.   **(1 mark)**

(b) State whether any of the water samples are pure, and justify your answer.

....

.... **(2 marks)**

5 Solders are alloys used to join copper pipes or electrical components together. Some 'lead-free' solders are mixtures of tin and silver. The table shows the melting points of tin, silver and a lead-free solder.

Explain how the data show that the lead-free solder is a mixture.

Substance	Melting point (°C)
tin	232
silver	962
lead-free solder	220–229

....

> Look at how the melting points are shown for each substance.

....

.... **(2 marks)**

Distillation

1 Which of the following is a suitable method to separate a mixture of two miscible liquids?

> Miscible liquids mix completely with each other.

☐ **A** filtration

☐ **B** simple distillation

☐ **C** fractional distillation

☐ **D** paper chromatography   **(1 mark)**

2 The apparatus shown in the diagram is used to separate the components of an ink.

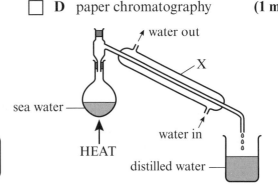

(a) (i) Name the apparatus labelled **X**.

> Water vapour goes in and droplets of water come out.

.... **(1 mark)**

(ii) State what happens to the temperature of the vapour from the sea water as it passes through apparatus **X**.

.... **(1 mark)**

 Guided

(b) Cold water passes through apparatus **X**. Explain what happens to the temperature of this water.

The temperature of the water .... because ....

....

.... **(2 marks)**

3 Ethanol boils at 78 °C and water boils at 100 °C. The apparatus shown in the diagram is used to separate a mixture of ethanol and water.

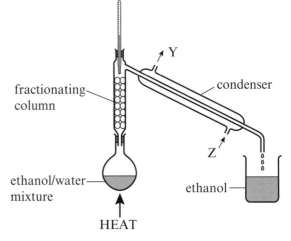

(a) Explain which liquid, ethanol or water, is collected first.

> Look again at the information given to you in the question.

....

.... **(2 marks)**

(b) Give a reason to explain why the cold water supply should be connected at **Z** rather than **Y**.

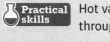 **Practical skills** Hot vapour from the ethanol–water mixture will pass from left to right through this apparatus.

....

.... **(1 mark)**

Filtration and crystallisation

1 A student filters a mixture of sand, salt and water. He collects the liquid that passes through the filter paper. Complete the table by placing a tick (✓) in the box against each correct statement.

> Do not place a cross against the incorrect statement(s) – you are asked to place only ticks in the table.

Statement	Tick (✓)
The liquid is water.	
The liquid is the filtrate.	
The salt is left behind as a residue.	
The sand is left behind as a residue.	

(2 marks)

> **Guided**

2 Potassium iodide solution reacts with lead nitrate solution. A mixture of potassium nitrate solution and insoluble yellow lead iodide forms. When this is filtered, solid lead iodide remains in the filter paper.

> Use the information in the question to decide whether each substance is solid, liquid or gas, or in aqueous solution. Few balanced equations use all four state symbols.

(a) Balance the equation below, and give the state symbols for each substance.

........$KI(aq)$ + $Pb(NO_3)_2$(........) $\rightarrow$ ....KNO_3(........) + PbI_2(........)   **(2 marks)**

(b) The yellow lead iodide is washed, with distilled water, while it is on the filter paper.

(i) State why the lead iodide does not pass through the filter paper.

.... **(1 mark)**

(ii) Suggest a reason to explain why the lead iodide is washed.

.... **(1 mark)**

3 A student decides to make pure, dry copper chloride crystals. She adds an excess of insoluble copper carbonate to dilute hydrochloric acid. Copper chloride solution forms.

(a) Name a suitable method to remove excess copper carbonate from the copper chloride solution.

> If a substance is in excess, some of it is left over when the reaction finishes.

.... **(1 mark)**

(b) The student leaves her copper chloride solution in a dish on a windowsill. Crystals gradually form.

(i) Describe what happens to the solution as the crystals of copper chloride form.

....

....

.... **(2 marks)**

(ii) Give a reason to explain why the student pours away the remaining solution, and then pats the crystals with filter paper.

.... **(1 mark)**

(c) The student could heat her copper chloride solution instead of leaving it on a windowsill. Describe one step that she should take to obtain large crystals rather than small ones.

> Think about how she needs to carry out this heating so she gets large crystals.

....

.... **(1 mark)**

Paper chromatography

1 Paper chromatography is used to determine whether an orange squash drink, **O**, contains an illegal food colouring, **X**.

Spots of each substance, and spots of three legal food colourings (**A**, **B** and **C**), are added to chromatography paper. The diagram shows the result of the chromatography experiment.

(a) Suggest a reason to explain why the start line is drawn using a pencil, rather than using ink.

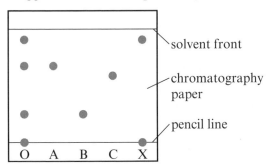

| solvent front
| chromatography paper
| pencil line

O   A   B   C   X

> **Practical skills** Think about the differences between pencil marks and pen marks.

.... **(1 mark)**

(b) Explain whether the orange squash, **O**, is a pure substance or a mixture.

> State if the orange squash is a pure substance or a mixture, then say why.

....

.... **(2 marks)**

(c) Identify which legal food colourings (**A**, **B** or **C**) are present in the orange squash.

.... **(1 mark)**

(d) Explain whether the orange squash contains the illegal food colouring, **X**.

....

.... **(2 marks)**

(e) Suggest a reason to explain why one of the substances in **X** remains on the pencil line.

> Remember that the paper is the stationary phase and the solvent the mobile phase, which runs through it.

.... **(1 mark)**

2 The diagram shows a chromatogram of a dye.

Calculate the R_f value of the spot in the chromatogram.

$$R_f = \frac{\text{distance travelled by a spot}}{\text{distance travelled by the solvent front}}$$

| solvent front

| start line   **(3 marks)**

Investigating inks

1 Paper chromatography is used to separate mixtures of coloured substances, such as those in inks.

(a) State two measurements that must be made so that an R_f value can be calculated.

> These are distances that must be measured on the finished chromatogram.

....

.... **(2 marks)**

(b) Suggest reasons to explain why these measurements are recorded to the nearest millimetre, rather than the nearest centimetre.

> **Maths skills** You must be able to use appropriate apparatus to make and record a range of measurements accurately.

....

.... **(2 marks)**

2 Simple distillation is used to separate a solvent from a solution.

(a) Suggest reasons to explain why the solution must be heated **gently**.

> This is not to do with a flammable solvent that might catch fire.

....

.... **(2 marks)**

(b) During distillation, the solvent vapour may condense slowly without the use of a condenser. State one hazard caused by carrying out distillation without a condenser.

> Remember that a hazard could harm something or someone, or could affect someone's health.

.... **(1 mark)**

3 A student investigates the composition of a sample of ballpoint pen ink. He uses propanone for the mobile phase in his paper chromatography. The diagram shows part of the label on a bottle of propanone.

> Irritating to eyes.
> May cause skin dryness.
> Vapour causes dizziness.
> Propanone CH_3COCH_3

(a) State one hazard of propanone, shown by the label but not described in words.

.... **(1 mark)**

> **Guided**

(b) Explain **two** precautions, other than eye protection, to control the risk of harm from propanone.

> You need to be able to use gases, liquids and solids safely and carefully.

The student should work in a fume cupboard because ....

....

The propanone causes skin dryness, so the student should ....

.... **(2 marks)**

Drinking water

1   Waste water and ground water can be treated to make it safe to drink. Which word correctly describes water that is safe for us to drink?

☐ **A** potable   ☐ **C** edible

☐ **B** fresh   ☐ **D** filtered   **(1 mark)**

2   Chlorine is a toxic gas that dissolves in water.

   (a) State why chlorine is used in water treatment.

| Your answer must be more precise than just 'to make it safe to drink'. |

   .... **(1 mark)**

> **Guided**

   (b) Drinking water contains low concentrations of dissolved chlorine. Suggest reasons to explain why this water is considered safe to drink, even though chlorine gas is toxic.

   The concentration of chlorine is high enough to ....

   but low enough so that it .... **(2 marks)**

3   Name the two stages in water treatment that are carried out before chlorine is added. Give a reason why each stage is carried out.

| You do not have to place the two stages in a correct order in this question. |

   name of stage: ....

   reason: ....

   name of stage: ....

   reason: .... **(4 marks)**

4   Explain why distilled water, rather than tap water, is used in chemical analysis.

> **Guided**

   Unlike tap water, distilled water does not contain ....

   These would .... **(2 marks)**

5   Drinking water in the UK comes from fresh water including rivers, lakes and reservoirs. In some countries drinking water may come from sea water instead.

   (a) Name a separation method used to separate water for drinking from sea water.

   .... **(1 mark)**

   (b) Suggest a reason to explain why producing drinking water from sea water is usually expensive.

   .... **(1 mark)**

6   Aluminium sulfate may be added during water treatment. It forms a precipitate of aluminium hydroxide, which traps small solid particles suspended in the water. Balance the equation for this reaction.

   $Al_2(SO_4)_3(aq) + ...H_2O(l) \rightarrow ....Al(OH)_3(s) + ...H_2SO_4(aq)$ **(1 mark)**

Extended response – Separating mixtures

*A cloudy pale-yellow mixture contains three substances (**A**, **B** and **C**).

The table shows some information about these substances.

Substance	Melting point (°C)	Boiling point (°C)	Notes
A	115	445	yellow, insoluble in **B** and **C**
B	–95	56	colourless, soluble in **C**
C	0	100	colourless, soluble in **B**

Devise a method to produce pure samples of each individual substance from the mixture.

> The command word **devise** means that you are being asked to plan or invent a procedure from existing principles or ideas. You do not have to imagine a complex method that goes beyond your GCSE studies.

You should use the information in the table in your answer, and explain why you have suggested each step.

> The separation methods covered at GCSE include simple distillation, fractional distillation, filtration, crystallisation and paper chromatography. You do not need to use them all to answer this question.

> Work out whether each substance is a solid, liquid or gas. Also work out whether they mix to form a solution. Then think about the properties that could be used to separate each substance from the others. How could you separate **A** from **B** and **C**, and **B** from **C**?

....

....

....

....

....

....

....

....

....

....

....

.... **(6 marks)**

> You should be able to describe an appropriate experimental technique to separate a mixture if you know the properties of the components of the mixture.

Acids and alkalis

1 Acids and alkalis in solution are sources of ions. Which of the following is correct?

☐ **A** Acids are a source of hydroxide ions, H^+.

☐ **B** Acids are a source of hydrogen ions, OH^-.

☐ **C** Alkalis are a source of hydrogen ions, H^+.

☐ **D** Alkalis are a source of hydroxide ions, OH^-. **(1 mark)**

2 A student adds a few drops of universal indicator solution to some dilute hydrochloric acid.

(a) The universal indicator solution is green before it is added to the acid. Explain what this tells you about the pH of the universal indicator solution.

....

.... **(2 marks)**

(b) Give the colour of the mixture formed by the universal indicator solution and dilute hydrochloric acid.

.... **(1 mark)**

3 A student heats some magnesium ribbon in air. It burns with a white flame and a white solid forms. The student then mixes the white solid with water in a test tube.

(a) Balance the equation for the reaction between magnesium and oxygen.

........$Mg + O_2 \rightarrow$ ....MgO

> The equation is balanced when the number of atoms of each element is the same on both sides.

(1 mark)

(b) Universal indicator solution turns purple when it is added to the mixture in the test tube. State what this tells you about the mixture.

.... **(1 mark)**

4 Complete the table by placing a tick (✓) in each correct box to show whether a substance is an acid or an alkali.

> You should be able to recall the formulae of elements and simple compounds.

Formula of substance	Type of substance	
	Acid	Alkali
NaOH		
HCl		
H_2SO_4		
NH_3		

(4 marks)

5 (a) Complete the table to show the colours of litmus, methyl orange and phenolphthalein at different pH values.

> Guided

> You should be able to recall the effect of acids and alkalis on these indicators.

Indicator	Colour at pH 14	Colour at pH 1
litmus		
methyl orange	yellow	red
phenolphthalein		

(2 marks)

(b) Predict the colour of litmus solution in pure water.

.... **(1 mark)**

Bases and alkalis

1 What forms when an acid reacts with a metal hydroxide?

    ☐ **A**   a salt only   ☐ **C**   a salt and hydrogen only

    ☐ **B**   a salt and water only   ☐ **D**   a salt and carbon dioxide only   **(1 mark)**

2 Sodium carbonate reacts with dilute nitric acid, forming three products.

    (a) Name the salt formed in this reaction.

    .... **(1 mark)**

    (b) Write a word equation for this reaction.

    .... **(1 mark)**

    (c) Describe two things that you would see when sodium carbonate powder is added to dilute nitric acid.

> You do not need to name any substances in your answer.

      1 ....

      2 .... **(2 marks)**

3 Calcium reacts with dilute hydrochloric acid. Bubbles of gas are given off and a colourless solution forms.

    (a) Name the colourless solution that forms.

    .... **(1 mark)**

    (b) Name the gas responsible for the bubbles.

    .... **(1 mark)**

4 Describe the chemical test for:

> **Practical skills**   Write down what you would do and what you would expect to observe.

    (a) carbon dioxide

    ....

    .... **(2 marks)**

    (b) hydrogen.

    ....

    .... **(2 marks)**

5 Zinc oxide is an example of a base.

    (a) Describe what is meant by a **base**.

      A base is any substance that reacts with ....

      to form a .... and .... only.   **(2 marks)**

    (b) State the general name for a **soluble** base.

    .... **(1 mark)**

    (c) Name the salt formed when zinc oxide reacts with dilute sulfuric acid.

    .... **(1 mark)**

Neutralisation

1 Acids react with alkalis to form salts and water only. Explain, in terms of reacting ions, how water forms in these neutralisation reactions.

Hydrogen ions, H⁺, from the .... react with

.... ions from the ....

to form ....   **(3 marks)**

2 Dilute hydrochloric acid, HCl, reacts with calcium oxide and calcium hydroxide.

(a) Balance the equation for the reaction of calcium oxide with dilute hydrochloric acid.

$$CaO + \text{.......}HCl \rightarrow CaCl_2 + H_2O$$ **(1 mark)**

(b) Write a balanced equation for the reaction of calcium hydroxide, $Ca(OH)_2$, with dilute hydrochloric acid.

> The substances formed are the same as those in the reaction between calcium oxide and hydrochloric acid.

.... **(2 marks)**

> You should be able to use appropriate apparatus and substances to measure the pH in different situations.

3 Limewater is calcium hydroxide solution. A student investigates what happens to the pH when he adds small portions of limewater to 25 cm³ of dilute hydrochloric acid in a flask. The table shows his results.

Volume of limewater added (cm³)	pH of the mixture in the flask
0	1.6
5	1.8
10	2.0
15	2.2
20	2.6
24	3.8
25	7.0
26	10.4
30	11.2
35	11.5
40	11.6

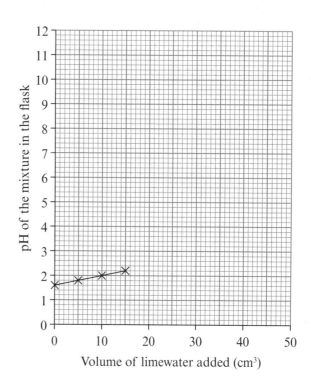

Complete the graph by plotting the remaining results.   **(2 marks)**

> **Maths skills** If you are asked to plot a graph, you need to mark the points accurately on the grid, then draw a line or curve of best fit. You must also work out a suitable scale and label the axes if this has not already been done for you.

Salts from insoluble bases

1   Iron(II) oxide is an insoluble base. It reacts with dilute sulfuric acid to form iron(II) sulfate solution and water:

$$FeO(s) + H_2SO_4(aq) \rightarrow FeSO_4(aq) + H_2O(l)$$

(a)   Explain why an excess of iron(II) oxide is added to the dilute sulfuric acid.

> If a reactant is in excess, some of it is left over when the reaction has finished.

....

.... **(2 marks)**

(b)   Suggest a reason to explain why the dilute sulfuric acid may be warmed before adding iron(II) oxide.

> What factors influence the rate of a reaction?

.... **(1 mark)**

(c)   Name the separation method needed to remove the excess iron(II) oxide.

.... **(1 mark)**

(d)   Name the process used to produce iron(II) sulfate crystals from the iron(II) sulfate solution.

.... **(1 mark)**

2   A student wants to prepare pure, dry crystals of copper sulfate. This is her method.

(a)   Name a suitable piece of apparatus to measure 25 cm³ of dilute sulfuric acid at step A.

> **Making copper sulfate crystals**
>
> **A** Put 25 cm³ of dilute sulfuric acid in a beaker.
> **B** Add several spatulas of copper oxide powder.
> **C** Pour the liquid from the beaker into an evaporating basin.
> **D** Heat the liquid using a blue Bunsen burner with the air hole fully open until all the water has boiled away.

.... **(1 mark)**

(b)   Describe **two** improvements that the student could make at step B, and give reasons for your answers.

improvement 1: ....

reason:..

improvement 2: ....

reason:.. **(4 marks)**

(c)   Describe **one** improvement that the student could make at step C, and give a reason for your answer.

> Think about whether there are any substances contaminating the copper sulfate solution.

improvement: ....

reason: .... **(2 marks)**

Salts from soluble bases

1 Which of the following is a suitable method for preparing a soluble salt from an acid and an alkali?

☐ **A** precipitation   ☐ **B** filtration   ☐ **C** titration   ☐ **D** distillation   **(1 mark)**

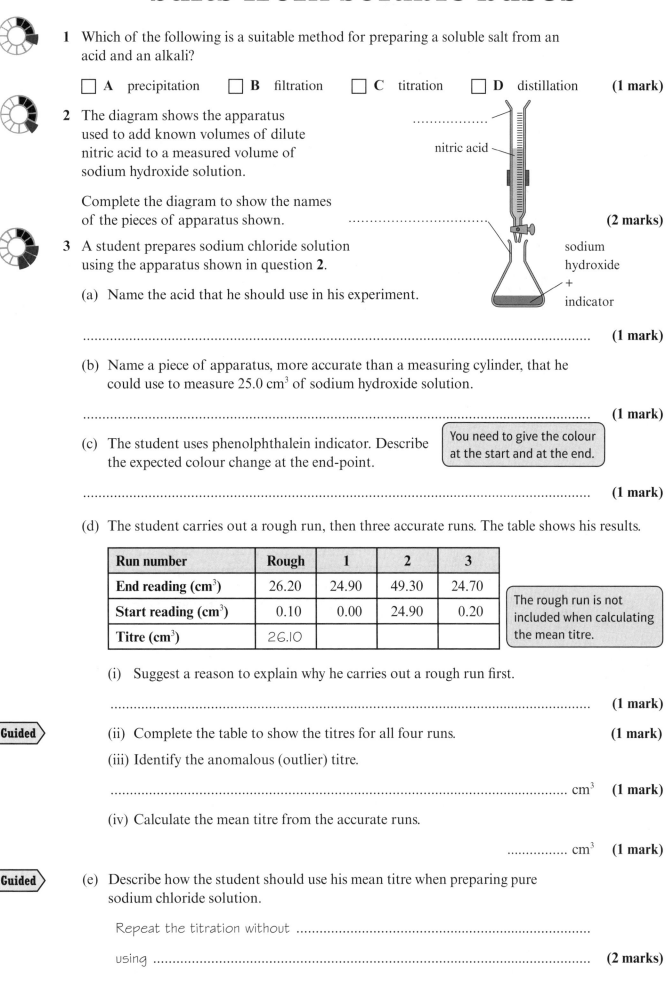

2 The diagram shows the apparatus used to add known volumes of dilute nitric acid to a measured volume of sodium hydroxide solution.

....

nitric acid

Complete the diagram to show the names of the pieces of apparatus shown.   **(2 marks)**

....

sodium hydroxide + indicator

3 A student prepares sodium chloride solution using the apparatus shown in question **2**.

(a) Name the acid that he should use in his experiment.

....   **(1 mark)**

(b) Name a piece of apparatus, more accurate than a measuring cylinder, that he could use to measure 25.0 cm^3 of sodium hydroxide solution.

....   **(1 mark)**

(c) The student uses phenolphthalein indicator. Describe the expected colour change at the end-point.

> You need to give the colour at the start and at the end.

....   **(1 mark)**

(d) The student carries out a rough run, then three accurate runs. The table shows his results.

Run number	Rough	1	2	3
End reading (cm^3)	26.20	24.90	49.30	24.70
Start reading (cm^3)	0.10	0.00	24.90	0.20
Titre (cm^3)	26.10			

> The rough run is not included when calculating the mean titre.

(i) Suggest a reason to explain why he carries out a rough run first.

....   **(1 mark)**

Guided (ii) Complete the table to show the titres for all four runs.   **(1 mark)**

(iii) Identify the anomalous (outlier) titre.

.... cm^3 **(1 mark)**

(iv) Calculate the mean titre from the accurate runs.

.... cm^3 **(1 mark)**

Guided (e) Describe how the student should use his mean titre when preparing pure sodium chloride solution.

Repeat the titration without ....

using ....   **(2 marks)**

35

Making insoluble salts

1 Potassium chloride is a metal chloride that is soluble in water. Which of the following metal chlorides is insoluble in water?

> You need to be able to recall the general rules for the solubility of common types of substances in water.

- ☐ **A** sodium chloride
- ☐ **B** silver chloride
- ☐ **C** copper chloride
- ☐ **D** zinc chloride   **(1 mark)**

2 Which of the following pairs contains one substance that is soluble in water and one that is insoluble in water?

- ☐ **A** lead chloride and barium sulfate
- ☐ **B** calcium nitrate and potassium hydroxide
- ☐ **C** aluminium hydroxide and copper carbonate
- ☐ **D** ammonium carbonate and calcium sulfate   **(1 mark)**

3 A student wants to produce insoluble calcium hydroxide.

(a) Name two solutions that, when mixed together, will produce a precipitate of calcium hydroxide.

> To make a precipitate XY, you can mix X nitrate with sodium Y.

solution 1: ....

solution 2: ....   **(2 marks)**

(b) Name the other product formed when the two solutions named in part (**a**) are mixed together.

....   **(1 mark)**

(c) Suggest a reason to explain why the student does not need to heat the solutions first.

> **Practical skills** Think about how quickly precipitation reactions happen, and what heating does to the rate of a reaction.

....   **(1 mark)**

4 Sodium carbonate, Na_2CO_3, and calcium chloride, $CaCl_2$, are soluble in water. Calcium carbonate, $CaCO_3$, is insoluble in water.

(a) Balance the equation for the reaction between sodium carbonate solution and calcium chloride solution. Include state symbols in your answer.

$Na_2CO_3(......) + CaCl_2(......) \rightarrow ...... NaCl(......) + CaCO_3(......)$ **(2 marks)**

(b) Describe how you would use solid sodium carbonate and solid calcium chloride to produce a pure, dry sample of calcium carbonate.

Guided

Add water to .... then mix.

Separate the precipitate of calcium carbonate using ....

Wash the .... using ....

then dry it by ....   **(4 marks)**

Extended response – Making salts

*Sodium chloride solution can be made from dilute hydrochloric acid and sodium hydroxide solution:

$$HCl(aq) + NaOH(aq) \rightarrow NaCl(aq) + H_2O(l)$$

Devise a titration experiment to find the exact volume of hydrochloric acid needed to neutralise 25.0 cm³ of sodium hydroxide solution. Explain how you would use the result from this experiment to obtain pure, dry, sodium chloride crystals.

It may help to plan your answers to questions similar to this one. For example, you could divide your answer here into three sections:

- setting up the apparatus ready for a titration, including where the reagents need to go
- carrying out the titration, including steps needed to obtain an accurate result
- producing sodium chloride crystals from sodium chloride solution.

....

....

....

....

....

....

....

....

....

....

....

....

....

....

....

....

....

....   **(6 marks)**

You should be able to describe how to carry out an acid–alkali titration using a burette, a pipette and a suitable indicator, to prepare a pure, dry salt.

Electrolysis

1   Under what conditions can an ionic compound conduct electricity?

> Molten substances are in the liquid state.

☐   **A**   only when it is molten

☐   **B**   when it is solid or molten

☐   **C**   when it is solid or dissolved in water

☐   **D**   when it is molten or dissolved in water   **(1 mark)**

2   Complete the table by placing a tick (✓) in each correct box to describe some features of electrolysis.

> You will need one tick in each row.

	Positively charged	Negatively charged
Anode		
Anion		
Cathode		
Cation		

(4 marks)

3   State what is meant by the term '**electrolyte**'.

> **Guided**

An electrolyte is an .... compound in the .... state

or ....   **(2 marks)**

4   In an electrolysis experiment, molten zinc bromide is decomposed.

Zinc forms at the cathode. Predict the product that forms at the anode.

....   **(1 mark)**

5   Sodium is extracted from molten sodium chloride, NaCl, by electrolysis. The reaction at one of the electrodes can be modelled as: $Na^+ + e^- \rightarrow Na$

State at which electrode, the positively or negatively charged electrode, this reaction happens. Give a reason for your answer using information from the equation.

> Look at the charge on the sodium ions.

....

....   **(1 mark)**

6   A student places a purple crystal of potassium manganate(VII), $KMnO_4$, on a damp piece of filter paper. She connects each end of the paper to a DC electricity supply.
A purple streak gradually moves to the left.

+ ⚬〜〜〜⚫— potassium manganate(VII) 〜〜〜⚬ −

> Potassium manganate(VII) contains manganate(VII) ions, MnO_4^-, and colourless potassium ions, K^+.

Explain why the purple streak moves to the left.

....

....   **(2 marks)**

Electrolysing solutions

1 The ions in copper chloride solution are:

- copper ions, Cu^{2+}
- chloride ions, Cl^-
- hydrogen ions, H^+
- hydroxide ions, OH^-

Copper chloride solution is electrolysed using a DC electricity supply.

(a) Which of these ions form from the water in the copper chloride solution?

☐ **A** H^+ and Cu^{2+} ions

☐ **B** H^+ and OH^- ions

☐ **C** H^+ ions only

☐ **D** OH^- ions only   **(1 mark)**

(b) Which of these ions will be attracted to the cathode during the electrolysis of copper chloride solution?

> The cathode is the negatively charged electrode.

☐ **A** Cl^- ions only

☐ **B** Cl^- ions and OH^- ions

☐ **C** H^+ ions only

☐ **D** H^+ and Cu^{2+} ions   **(1 mark)**

(c) Predict the substance formed at the cathode during the electrolysis of concentrated copper chloride solution.

.... **(1 mark)**

2 The electrolysis of concentrated sodium chloride solution, NaCl(aq), produces two useful gases.

(a) Write the formulae of all the ions present in a concentrated sodium chloride solution.

> You should be able to recall the formulae of ions.

.... **(2 marks)**

(b) Predict the gas that forms at:

(i) the anode .... **(1 mark)**

(ii) the cathode. .... **(1 mark)**

3 Water, acidified with sulfuric acid, can be decomposed by electrolysis. Complete the table by writing the correct product into each box.

Electrode	Product formed
anode	
cathode	

(2 marks)

4 Oxygen is produced at the anode during the electrolysis of sodium sulfate solution.

Name, or give the formula of, the ions present in this solution that are discharged to form oxygen.

> Which negatively charged ions will be present in this solution?

.... **(1 mark)**

 **Practical skills** # Investigating electrolysis

A student researched the different types of electrode used for electrolysis. This is what he found out.

> **Electrodes**
>
> Electrodes can be inert or non-inert. Graphite electrodes are inert electrodes – they just provide a surface for electrode reactions to happen. Copper electrodes are non-inert electrodes for the electrolysis of copper sulfate solution. Their copper atoms may form copper ions, causing the electrode to lose mass.

 1 Oxygen forms during the electrolysis of copper sulfate solution using graphite electrodes.

> Look at the information that the student discovered.

(a) State whether the electrodes are inert or non-inert in this electrolysis reaction.

.... **(1 mark)**

(b) Explain at which electrode (anode or cathode) oxygen will be produced.

....

.... **(2 marks)**

 2 The electrolysis of copper sulfate solution, using copper electrodes, is used to purify copper. During electrolysis, the copper anode loses mass. The copper cathode gains mass because copper is deposited.

A student investigates the gain in mass by a copper cathode. She runs each experiment for the same time, but changes the current. She measures the mass of the cathode before and after electrolysis. The graph shows her results.

(a) Identify the variable controlled by the student in her experiment.

> Variables are factors that can be measured or observed.

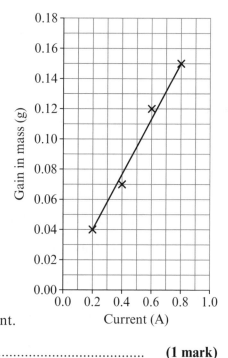

.... **(1 mark)**

(b) Identify the dependent variable in the student's experiment.

.... **(1 mark)**

(c) State whether the electrodes are inert or non-inert in this experiment, and justify your answer.

....

.... **(1 mark)**

(d) Calculate the gradient of the line of best fit. Give your answer to two significant figures.

> Guided

change on the y-axis = 0.15 – 0.04 = ...

change on the x-axis = ... – .... = ...

gradient = ...

= .... g/A

> A linear relationship such as this can be represented by: $y = mx + c$
> m is the gradient and c is the intercept on the vertical axis (y-axis). The gradient equals the change on the y-axis, divided by the change on the x-axis.

(3 marks)

Extended response – Electrolysis

*A student carries out two experiments using copper chloride, $CuCl_2$.

In experiment 1, the student places two graphite electrodes into solid copper chloride powder in a beaker. She then connects the electrodes to a DC electricity supply and records any changes.

For experiment 2, the student disconnects the DC supply, then adds some water to dissolve the copper chloride. She reconnects the electrodes to the DC supply and records any changes.

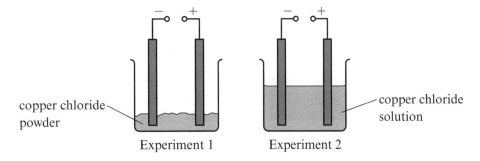

copper chloride powder

Experiment 1   Experiment 2

copper chloride solution

The table shows the student's results.

Experiment	Observations at the cathode (−)	Observations at the anode (+)
1	no visible change	no visible change
2	brown solid forms on the electrode	bubbles of a pale yellow–green gas released

Explain the differences between the results shown in the table for experiments 1 and 2. You should include a balanced equation for the overall reaction in your answer.

> Explain why copper chloride powder does not conduct electricity, and then explain why copper chloride solution does conduct electricity. Name the substances responsible for the student's observations at each electrode during experiment 2.

....

....

....

....

....

....

....

....

....

....   **(6 marks)**

> Explain, in terms of the ions in the copper chloride solution, why each substance forms.

The reactivity series

1   Four metals (**W**, **X**, **Y** and **Z**) are added to cold water and to dilute hydrochloric acid.
The table shows what happens.

Metal	Observations in water	Observations in dilute hydrochloric acid
W	slow bubbling	very fast bubbling
X	no visible change	no visible change
Y	fast bubbling	very fast bubbling
Z	no visible change	slow bubbling

(a) Which of the following shows the order of reactivity, from most reactive to least reactive metal?

☐ **A** W, Y, X, Z   ☐ **C** Y, W, X, Z

☐ **B** X, Z, W, Y   ☐ **D** Y, W, Z, X   **(1 mark)**

(b) The concentration of hydrochloric acid is kept the same each time. Give two other variables that should be kept the same in each experiment so that the reactivity of the metals can be compared.

....

....   **(2 marks)**

2   Name one common metal that does not react with dilute acids.

> Metals that are less reactive than hydrogen do not react with dilute acids.

....   **(1 mark)**

3   Magnesium reacts slowly with cold water to produce magnesium hydroxide, $Mg(OH)_2$, and a gas.

> This flammable gas is produced when any metal reacts with water or dilute acids.

(a) (i)   Name the gas produced in the reaction.

....   **(1 mark)**

(ii)   Describe the chemical test used to identify the gas produced in the reaction.

....

....   **(2 marks)**

(b) Name the compound formed when magnesium reacts with steam, rather than cold water.

....   **(1 mark)**

4   Aluminium is protected from contact with water by a natural layer of aluminium oxide, Al_2O_3. This means that aluminium does not react with water, even though it is a reactive metal. However, aluminium does react with dilute acids, such as dilute sulfuric acid.

(a) Balance the equation for the reaction between aluminium oxide and dilute sulfuric acid.

$$Al_2O_3(s) + ...H_2SO_4(aq) \rightarrow Al_2(SO_4)_3(aq) + ...H_2O(l)$$ **(1 mark)**

> Guided

(b) There is no immediate visible change when aluminium is added to dilute sulfuric acid. Bubbling then starts and gets increasingly fast. Suggest reasons that explain these observations.

To begin with, the acid reacts with ....

but, once this has gone, it reacts with ....   **(2 marks)**

Metal displacement reactions

1 Copper can displace silver from silver nitrate solution. Copper nitrate solution also forms in the reaction.

> Which metal, copper or silver, is the more reactive of the two metals?

(a) Give a reason to explain why copper can displace silver from silver salts in solution.

.... **(1 mark)**

(b) Balance the equation for the reaction, and include state symbols.

$Cu(........) + ... AgNO_3(aq) \rightarrow ....Ag(s) + Cu(NO_3)_2(........)$ **(2 marks)**

2 A student investigates the reactivities of four metals, copper, magnesium, zinc and X. She adds pieces of magnesium ribbon to solutions of the nitrates of each metal. She then removes and examines each piece of magnesium ribbon after a few minutes. The table shows her results.

Experiment	Solution used	Observations
1	copper nitrate	brown coating on the magnesium ribbon
2	magnesium nitrate	no visible change
3	zinc nitrate	grey coating on the magnesium ribbon
4	X nitrate	grey coating on the magnesium ribbon

(a) Name the substance found in the brown coating on the magnesium ribbon in Experiment 1.

.... **(1 mark)**

(b) Why is there no visible change when magnesium nitrate solution is used in Experiment 2.

.... **(1 mark)**

(c) The student repeats the experiment with metal X instead of magnesium.

Experiment	Solution used	Observations
5	copper nitrate	brown coating on the piece of metal X
6	magnesium nitrate	no visible change
7	zinc nitrate	grey coating on the piece of metal X
8	X nitrate	no visible change

(i) Use the results shown in both tables to place the **two most reactive** metals in order of **decreasing** reactivity.

....

.... **(1 mark)**

(ii) Describe one experiment needed to find the order of reactivity of the other two metals.

....

.... **(2 marks)**

3 The thermite reaction makes molten iron for welding railway lines:

$2Al(s) + Fe_2O_3(s) \rightarrow Al_2O_3(s) + 2Fe(l)$

Explain what this reaction shows about the relative reactivity of aluminium and iron.

....

.... **(2 marks)**

Explaining metal reactivity

1 Give the meaning of the term 'cation'.

> **Guided**

A cation is a .... charged ion.   **(1 mark)**

2 Calcium is a reactive metal. It reacts vigorously with dilute hydrochloric acid to form calcium chloride solution and hydrogen gas:

$Ca(s) + 2HCl(aq) \rightarrow CaCl_2(aq) + H_2(g)$

(a) The formula for a chloride ion is Cl^-. Deduce the formula for a calcium ion.

> Remember that the overall charge in $CaCl_2$ will be 0.

.... **(1 mark)**

> **Guided**

(b) Describe what happens when a calcium atom becomes a calcium ion.

> Mention how many electrons are lost and from where.

.... electrons are lost from the .... **(2 marks)**

(c) The table shows a reactivity series for the metals. Hydrogen is a non-metal. It is included for comparison.

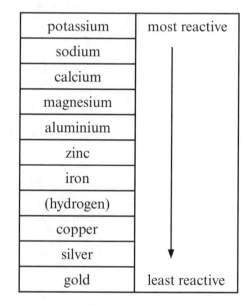

potassium	most reactive
sodium	
calcium	
magnesium	
aluminium	
zinc	
iron	
(hydrogen)	
copper	
silver	
gold	least reactive

> The more easily a metal's atoms form cations, the more reactive the metal is.

Identify the metal that:

(i) forms cations most easily   **(1 mark)**

....

(ii) forms cations least easily.

....

(1 mark)

(d) Identify a metal that will **not** react with dilute acids.

> Look at the position of hydrogen (a non-metal) in the reactivity series.

.... **(1 mark)**

3 Zinc displaces copper from copper sulfate solution:

$$Zn(s) + CuSO_4(aq) \rightarrow ZnSO_4(aq) + Cu(s)$$

Explain this reaction in terms of the tendency to form cations.

....

....

.... **(2 marks)**

Metal ores

1   Some metals are found in the Earth's crust as uncombined metals. Which of these
metals is found uncombined in the Earth's crust?

☐ **A** potassium   ☐ **C** gold

☐ **B** zinc   ☐ **D** aluminium   **(1 mark)**

2   Tungsten metal is extracted by heating tungsten oxide, WO_3, in a stream of
hydrogen gas, H_2:

$$WO_3 + 3H_2 \rightarrow W + 3H_2O$$

(a) What happens in this reaction?

☐ **A** Tungsten oxide is reduced.   ☐ **C** Tungsten is oxidised.

☐ **B** Hydrogen is reduced.   ☐ **D** Water is oxidised.   **(1 mark)**

(b) Suggest a reason to explain
why this process is hazardous.

> Look at the reactants and products – could any
> of them cause harm to people or objects?

.... **(1 mark)**

3   Metals are extracted from their ores. Give the meaning of the term '**ore**'.

> **Guided**

A rock or mineral that contains enough ....

to make its extraction .... **(2 marks)**

4   Tin is produced when tin oxide is heated with carbon.

(a) Complete the word equation for the reaction.

tin oxide + carbon → .... + ... **(2 marks)**

(b) Explain whether carbon is oxidised
or reduced in this reaction.

> Think about the gain or loss of
> oxygen in the reaction.

....

.... **(2 marks)**

5   Corrosion occurs when a metal oxidises, and this process continues. For example,
sodium is shiny when it is freshly cut, but a dull layer of sodium oxide forms quickly
when sodium is exposed to air.

(a) Suggest a reason to explain why sodium metal is stored in oil.

.... **(1 mark)**

(b) Give a reason to explain why copper oxidises slowly unless it is heated strongly.

....

.... **(1 mark)**

Iron and aluminium

1 The table shows a reactivity series for the metals.
Name a metal in the table that:

(a) is more reactive than carbon.

.... **(1 mark)**

(b) could be extracted from its ore by heating with carbon.

.... **(1 mark)**

sodium	most reactive
calcium	
magnesium	
(carbon)	
lead	
copper	least reactive

2 Metals are extracted from their ores in different ways. They may be extracted either by heating with carbon or by electrolysis. Iron is extracted from iron oxide by heating with carbon.

(a) Complete this word equation for the extraction of iron.

iron oxide + carbon → .... + ... **(2 marks)**

(b) State why iron can be extracted from iron oxide by heating with carbon.

> Think about the reactivity series.

.... **(1 mark)**

(c) State whether iron oxide is oxidised or reduced in this reaction, and give a reason for your answer.

.... **(1 mark)**

3 Bauxite is an aluminium ore. It contains aluminium oxide, Al_2O_3.
Aluminium is extracted from purified aluminium oxide by electrolysis.

(a) Give a reason why electrolysis is more expensive than heating with carbon.

> Think about the amount of energy involved in each method of extraction.

.... **(1 mark)**

(b) Predict the products formed at each electrode during the electrolysis of aluminium oxide.

> The cathode is the negatively charged electrode.

(i) at the cathode: .... **(1 mark)**

(ii) at the anode: .... **(1 mark)**

(c) The anodes are made from graphite, a form of carbon. Suggest a reason to explain why the anodes must be replaced frequently.

.... **(1 mark)**

4 Zinc could be extracted either by heating zinc oxide with carbon or by electrolysis of molten zinc oxide. Explain which method is mostly likely to be used.

> The method chosen is related to the position of a metal in the reactivity series and the cost of extracting it.

> Guided >

Zinc is most likely to be extracted by ....

....

because ....

.... **(2 marks)**

Recycling metals

1 Complete the table by placing a tick (✓) in the box against each **disadvantage** of recycling metals.

Feature of recycling metals	Disadvantage (✓)
Used metal items must be collected.	
The use of finite resources is decreased.	
Different metals must be sorted.	
Metals can be melted down.	

> Do not place a cross against the incorrect statement(s) – you are asked to place only ticks in the table.

(2 marks)

2 Metal ores are removed from the ground in large amounts by quarrying. This may involve using explosives to break up the rock, and large machinery and vehicles to carry the rock away. Give **two** ways in which quarrying can damage the local environment.

1: ....

2: .... **(2 marks)**

3 Around 90% of the lead produced each year is used in traditional 'lead acid' batteries for cars and other vehicles. About 70% of the lead used each year is recycled lead.

> **Guided**

(a) Describe an advantage of recycling lead from lead acid batteries, rather than recycling lead from general scrap metal waste.

> Think about how different metals are obtained from scrap metal waste.

Most lead for recycling is found in ....

so lead does not need to be .... **(2 marks)**

(b) Describe **two** advantages of recycling metals, rather than extracting them from their compounds.

1: ....

2: .... **(2 marks)**

4 Some food cans are made from aluminium. Others are made from steel (an iron alloy) coated with tin. The table shows some information about these three metals.

Metal	Abundance in the Earth's crust (%)	Cost of 1 tonne of metal (£)	Energy saved by recycling (%)
iron	6.3	500	70
tin	0.00022	16 500	75
aluminium	8.2	1500	94

(a) Identify the metal for which the most energy is saved by recycling.

> Use information from the table.

.... **(1 mark)**

(b) Give **two** reasons why it may be more important to recycle tin, rather than iron or aluminium. Use information from the table.

1: ....

2: .... **(2 marks)**

Life-cycle assessments

Guided

1 A life-time assessment for a manufactured product involves considering its effect on the environment at all stages.

The table shows the main steps involved in a life-time assessment. Give the correct order by writing the numbers 1 to 4 in the correct boxes, where step 1 is the first.

Step number	Process
	manufacturing the product
	obtaining raw materials
4	disposing of the product
	using the product

(1 mark)

Guided

2 Manufacturers can make glass bottles with thinner walls than in the past. A bottle for a fizzy drink had a mass of 0.24 kg in 1996 but a mass of 0.20 kg in 2016.

(a) 16.5 MJ/kg of glass is used in their manufacture.

(i) Calculate the energy, in MJ, needed to make one bottle in 1996.

energy = 16.5 × 0.24

= .... MJ **(1 mark)**

(ii) Calculate the energy, in MJ, needed to make one bottle in 2016.

.... MJ **(1 mark)**

Guided

(b) Carbon dioxide, CO_2, is a greenhouse gas. The manufacture of glass bottles causes the emission of 1.2 kg of CO_2/kg glass. Calculate the difference, between 1996 and 2016, in the mass of carbon dioxide emitted when one bottle is made.

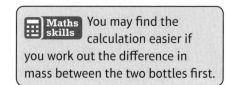

Maths skills You may find the calculation easier if you work out the difference in mass between the two bottles first.

difference in mass between bottles in 1996 and 2016 = 0.24 − 0.20

= .... kg

difference in the mass of CO_2 emitted = ... kg **(2 marks)**

3 Window frames may be made from either PVC (a polymer) or wood. The table shows some information from a life-cycle assessment of a window frame.

Process	Energy used (MJ)	
	PVC frame	**Wooden frame**
producing the material	12.0	4.0
making the frame	3.0	3.6
transport and installation	4.2	4.8
maintenance	0.3	1.5
disposal in landfill	0.7	0.8

(a) Identify the stage in the life cycle of each window frame that is responsible for the most energy use.

PVC frame: ....

wooden frame: .... **(1 mark)**

(b) Explain, using data in the table, which type of frame is likely to have the lower environmental impact **when in use**.

....

.... **(2 marks)**

Extended response – Reactivity of metals

*Magnesium forms cations more readily than copper. A spatula of magnesium powder mixed with a spatula of copper oxide powder is heated strongly on a steel lid. Magnesium oxide and copper are produced:

$$\text{magnesium} + \text{copper oxide} \rightarrow \text{magnesium oxide} + \text{copper}$$
$$Mg(s) + CuO(s) \rightarrow MgO(s) + Cu(s)$$

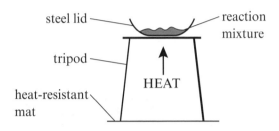

The reaction shows that magnesium is more reactive than copper. It is a very vigorous reaction. Energy is transferred to the surroundings by light and heating, and hot powder escapes into the air.

Devise an experiment, based on this method, to investigate the relative reactivity of copper, iron and zinc. In your answer, describe the results that you expect, and explain how you would use them to deduce the order of reactivity. Explain how you would control the risks of harm in the investigation.

> Think about how many combinations of a metal powder and a metal oxide powder you will need to test.
>
> One way to show these combinations, and the expected results, is to make a completed results table.

....

....

....

....

....

....

....

....

....

....

.... **(6 marks)**

> You should be able to evaluate the risks in a practical procedure, and suggest suitable precautions for a range of practicals (not just those mentioned in the specification).

Transition metals

1 Iron is a transition metal. Which of these is a property of pure iron?

☐ **A** It has a low melting point.

☐ **B** It is a poor conductor of electricity.

☐ **C** It has a high density.

☐ **D** It is brittle.

(1 mark)

2 Describe where the transition metals are found in the periodic table.

Guided

between groups ....

in the .... part of the periodic table

(2 marks)

3 The table shows the appearance of mixtures of water and four different metal compounds (**A**, **B**, **C** and **D**).

Metal hydroxide	Appearance of mixture
A	colourless solution
B	pale-green precipitate
C	white precipitate
D	dark-blue solution

(a) Identify the compounds of transition metals.

Write the letter or letters below.

.... **(1 mark)**

(b) Give a reason for your answer to part (**a**).

.... **(1 mark)**

4 The table shows the melting points of five metal elements (**A**, **B**, **C**, **D** and **E**).

Metal	A	B	C	D	E
Melting point (°C)	328	1244	98	420	232

(a) Identify the element that is likely to be a transition metal.

.... **(1 mark)**

(b) Give a reason for your answer to part (**a**).

.... **(1 mark)**

5 In the Haber process, nitrogen reacts with hydrogen to make ammonia. Iron, Fe, increases the rate of this reaction without being changed chemically or in mass.

(a) Name the type of substance that can increase the rate of reaction in this way.

.... **(1 mark)**

(b) Suggest a reason to explain why osmium, Os, has the same effect on the Haber process as iron does.

Where are these elements placed in the periodic table?

.... **(1 mark)**

Rusting

1 Rusting is the corrosion of iron. What type of reaction happens when iron rusts?

☐ **A** displacement

☐ **B** decomposition

☐ **C** combustion

☐ **D** oxidation   **(1 mark)**

2 (a) Name the **two** substances needed for iron to rust.

.... **(2 marks)**

> **Guided**

(b) Name the iron compound that forms when iron rusts.

hydrated iron ....**(1 mark)**

3 The rusting of iron and steel objects can be prevented in different ways.

> **Guided**

(a) Explain how oiling stops a steel bicycle chain rusting.

The layer of oil stops ....

.... **(2 marks)**

(b) A new camera is packaged in a box with a small bag of crystals.

The label on this bag is shown on the right.

| 'Supabzorb' |
| DESICCANT |
| Silica gel |

(i) Explain why the bag protects the camera's moving steel parts from rusting.

> What substance, needed for rusting to happen, does a desiccant absorb?

....

.... **(2 marks)**

(ii) Suggest a reason to explain why the camera parts were not painted to prevent rusting.

.... **(1 mark)**

4 Steel screws for use on boats may be electroplated with nickel. This improves the resistance to corrosion of the screws. Give one other reason why metal objects may be electroplated.

.... **(1 mark)**

5 Car body panels, made from steel, are usually coated with zinc before they are painted. The zinc acts as another barrier in case the paint is damaged. It continues to prevent rusting, even if the zinc layer is also damaged.

(a) Give the name of the type of rust prevention shown by a damaged layer of zinc.

.... **(1 mark)**

> **Guided**

(b) Explain how this type of rust prevention works.

Zinc is more ....

so zinc oxidises .... **(2 marks)**

Alloys

1   Brass is made by dissolving hot pieces of zinc in molten copper, and then letting the mixture cool and solidify. What type of substance is brass?

> Answer D cannot be correct because metals such as zinc and copper are extracted from ores.

☐ **A**   a compound   ☐ **C**   an alloy

☐ **B**   an element   ☐ **D**   an ore   **(1 mark)**

2   Give **two** reasons why gold is used to make jewellery.

> Think about the physical and chemical properties of gold that make it suitable for use as a metal for jewellery.

1: ....

2: .... **(2 marks)**

3   Iron is alloyed with other metals to produce alloy steels. These metals are often more useful than pure iron. For example, they may be stronger. State one way in which alloy steels can be more useful than pure iron.

> Think about the properties and uses of alloy steels compared with pure iron.

....

(1 mark)

4   The table shows some information about an aluminium alloy and copper.

Metal	Relative strength	Relative electrical conductivity	Corrosion resistance	Density (kg/m^3)
aluminium alloy	2.2	0.6	good	2700
copper	1.0	1.0	good	8920

Describe two reasons why the alloy, rather than copper, is more suitable for overhead electricity cables.

> 🖩 **Maths skills** Relative values have no units. Relative strength and electrical conductivity are compared with copper here.

1: ....

....

2: ....

.... **(2 marks)**

5   The diagrams show the structures of pure aluminium, and an alloy of aluminium and magnesium.

Guided

Explain, in terms of their structures, why the alloy is stronger than pure aluminium.

pure aluminium   alloy

The layers of atoms in aluminium can ....

Magnesium atoms are ....

so the layers in the alloy .... **(3 marks)**

Extended response –
Alloys and corrosion

*Some metal cutlery is marked with the letters EPNS. This stands for electroplated nickel silver.

The cutlery itself is made from 'nickel silver', an alloy of nickel, zinc and copper. Electroplating is used to deposit a thin layer of pure silver onto the cutlery. This improves both the cutlery's appearance and its resistance to corrosion.

Describe how you could electroplate a nickel silver spoon with silver. In your answer, you should name a suitable electrolyte, and identify the anode and cathode.

> When thinking about a suitable electrolyte, it helps to recall that all metal nitrates are soluble in water.

> A simple labelled diagram can save a lot of words when you answer a question such as this.

....

....

....

....

....

....

....

....

....

....

....

....

....

....

....

....

.... (6 marks)

Practical skills   Accurate titrations

1 Suggest a reason to explain why universal indicator solution should **not** be used in titrations.

> Think about how universal indicator solution changes colour when an acid or alkali is added slowly to it.

.... **(1 mark)**

2 An acid–base indicator is used when sodium hydroxide solution is titrated with dilute hydrochloric acid. In this titration, the acid is added to the alkali in a flask. The end-point is when the indicator changes colour.

(a) Name a suitable indicator solution for this titration.

.... **(1 mark)**

(b) Describe the colour change for the indicator named in part (a) at the end-point in this titration.

> You need to give the indicator's colour in alkaline solution **and** in acidic solution.

.... **(1 mark)**

3 In a titration, it is common to add a 25.0 cm³ portion of the alkali solution to a conical flask.

> Guided

Describe how to add 25.0 cm³ of a liquid to a conical flask accurately and safely for a titration.

The accurate apparatus needed is a ....

To use it accurately, I would ....

The safety apparatus needed is a .... **(3 marks)**

4 The diagrams show parts of the burette during a titration.

(a) Give the readings to the nearest 0.05 cm³.

> The readings should be taken at the bottom of the meniscus, not where the liquid touches the sides.

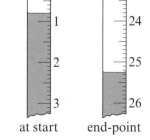

at start   end-point

start reading: ....

end-point reading: .... **(2 marks)**

> Guided

(b) Calculate the titre using your answers to part (a).

titre = (end-point reading) – (start reading) = ...

= .... **(1 mark)**

5 A student carries out a titration. State why he:

(a) swirls the conical flask containing the alkali solution while adding dilute acid from the burette

.... **(1 mark)**

(b) adds acid drop by drop near the end-point

.... **(1 mark)**

(c) reads the burette at eye level.

.... **(1 mark)**

Percentage yield

1 When it is heated, copper carbonate decomposes to form copper oxide and carbon dioxide. A student heats some copper carbonate. The table shows her results.

Substance	Mass (g)
copper carbonate used	2.5
copper oxide obtained	1.4

What was the actual yield of copper oxide in this experiment?

☐ **A**   1.1 g   ☐ **B**   1.4 g

☐ **C**   2.5 g   ☐ **D**   3.9 g   **(1 mark)**

2 State what is meant by the term '**theoretical yield**'.

Guided

the maximum mass of product ....

.... **(1 mark)**

3 Magnesium reacts with oxygen to form magnesium oxide: $2Mg(s) + O_2(g) \rightarrow 2MgO(s)$

Guided

The theoretical yield when heating 2.4 g of magnesium is 4.0 g. In an experiment with 2.4 g of magnesium, the actual yield was only 3.0 g of magnesium oxide.

(a) The percentage yield in this reaction could be reduced by a side reaction, such as magnesium reacting with nitrogen. Give two other reasons why the percentage yield in this experiment is not 100%.

The reaction might not ....

and some magnesium oxide could be .... **(2 marks)**

(b) Calculate the percentage yield for this experiment.

$$\text{percentage yield} = \frac{\text{actual yield}}{\text{theoretical yield}} \times 100$$

percentage yield = ... × 100

= .... **(2 marks)**

4 (a) Calculate the percentage yield for a reaction in which the theoretical yield is 2.86 g and the actual yield is 2.43 g.

.... **(2 marks)**

(b) Calculate the actual yield for a reaction in which the percentage yield is 70% and the theoretical yield is 50 g.

> 🖩 **Maths skills** You will need to rearrange the expression given in question 3 for calculating percentage yields.

.... **(2 marks)**

Atom economy

1 Ethene reacts with steam to form ethanol: $C_2H_4(g) + H_2O(g) \rightarrow C_2H_5OH(g)$

What is the atom economy of this reaction? You do not need to carry out a calculation.

> Answer D cannot be correct because atom economy cannot be greater than 100%.

☐ **A** 100%

☐ **C** 50%

☐ **B** 66.7%

☐ **D** 150%   **(1 mark)**

> Guided

2 Potassium nitrate, KNO_3, may be used as a fertiliser. It is manufactured by reacting potassium hydroxide solution with dilute nitric acid:

$KOH(aq) + HNO_3(aq) \rightarrow KNO_3(aq) + H_2O(l)$

Calculate the atom economy of this process. Give your answer to **three significant figures**.

(M_r of $KNO_3 = 101$ and M_r of $H_2O = 18$)

> **Maths skills** Look at the fourth digit from the left in your answer. Round the third digit up if the fourth digit is 5 or more.

total M_r of desired product, KNO_3 = ...

total M_r of all products = 101 + 18 = ...

atom economy = (.............../...............) × 100 = ...   **(2 marks)**

> Guided

3 Iron can be extracted from iron(III) oxide by heating with carbon:

$Fe_2O_3(s) + 3C(s) \rightarrow 2Fe(l) + 3CO(g)$

Calculate the atom economy of this process. Give your answer to **three significant figures**.

(A_r of Fe = 56 and M_r of CO = 28)

> Calculate the **total** A_r and M_r values of the products.

total M_r of desired product, Fe = 2 × 56 = ...

total M_r of all products = (2 × 56) + (3 × 28) = ...

atom economy = (.............../...............) × 100 = ...   **(2 marks)**

> Guided

4 Ethanol can be manufactured by fermentation:

glucose   →   ethanol   + carbon dioxide

$C_6H_{12}O_6(aq) \rightarrow 2C_2H_5OH(g) + 2CO_2(g)$

Calculate the atom economy of fermentation to produce ethanol. Give your answer to **three significant figures**.
(A_r of H = 1, A_r of C = 12 and A_r of O = 16)

> Calculate the relative formula masses, M_r, of both products first.

M_r of C_2H_5OH = (2 × 12) + (6 × 1) + 16 = ...

M_r of CO_2 = ...

total M_r of desired product = ...

total M_r of all products = ...

atom economy = (.............../...............) × 100 = ...   **(3 marks)**

Exam skills – Chemical calculations

Oxygen was manufactured in the past using the Brin process. This process happens in two stages:

Stage 1: barium oxide is heated to 500 °C. It reacts with oxygen in the air to form barium peroxide:

$$2BaO(s) + O_2(g) \rightarrow 2BaO_2(s)$$

Stage 2: barium peroxide is heated to over 800 °C, which releases oxygen:

$$2BaO_2(s) \rightarrow 2BaO(s) + O_2(g)$$

Barium oxide formed in stage 2 could then be used again for stage 1.

(a) This part of the question is about stage 1 of the Brin process.

   (i) Calculate the relative formula mass, M_r, of barium oxide, BaO.

   (A_r of Ba = 137 and A_r of O = 16)

   .... **(1 mark)**

   (ii) Calculate the relative formula mass, M_r, of oxygen gas.

   .... **(1 mark)**

(b) Calculate the maximum mass of oxygen that will react with 250 g of barium oxide. Give your answer to three significant figures.

   .... **(2 marks)**

(c) Give a reason why the atom economy of stage 1 is 100%.

   .... **(1 mark)**

(d) Calculate the atom economy of stage 2 for producing oxygen. Use your relative formula masses calculated in part (a) to help you. Give your answer to two significant figures.

   .... **(2 marks)**

(e) Carbon dioxide in the air reacts with barium oxide to form barium carbonate. This unwanted side reaction reduces the amount of barium oxide available to react, and so reduces the yield of oxygen.

   (i) Give another reason why the actual yield of oxygen may be less than the theoretical yield.

   .... **(1 mark)**

   (ii) A chemist used the Brin process to obtain some oxygen from the air. The theoretical yield of oxygen was 24.7 kg but the actual yield was 21.0 kg. Calculate the percentage yield.

   .... **(2 marks)**

(f) Barium oxide reacts with water to form barium hydroxide solution:
   $$BaO(s) + H_2O(l) \rightarrow Ba(OH)_2(aq)$$

   2.50 dm³ of a barium hydroxide solution contains 21.3 g of barium hydroxide.

   > You may have opportunities to carry out calculations involving different aspects of chemistry.

   Calculate its concentration in g dm⁻³.

   .... **(2 marks)**

The Haber process

1 In the Haber process, nitrogen and hydrogen react together to form ammonia:

$$N_2(g) + 3H_2(g) \rightleftharpoons 2NH_3(g)$$

	Nitrogen	Hydrogen
☐ A	air	hydrochloric acid
☐ B	natural gas	air
☐ C	sea water	natural gas
☐ D	air	natural gas

(a) Which row correctly shows the raw materials for nitrogen and hydrogen?

(1 mark)

(b) Give the meaning of the symbol $\rightleftharpoons$ in the balanced equation.

.... **(1 mark)**

2 The conditions used in the Haber process are carefully controlled to achieve an acceptable yield of ammonia in an acceptable time.

(a) State the temperature and pressure used in the Haber process.

temperature: .... °C

pressure: .... atmospheres **(2 marks)**

(b) Explain why iron is added to the reactor used in the Haber process.

> Iron affects the reaction but is not a reactant or a product.

....

.... **(2 marks)**

3 Dilute ethanoic acid reacts with ethanol. Ethyl ethanoate and water form in the reaction:

> You may see familiar chemistry in an unfamiliar context, like this one.

ethanoic acid + ethanol $\rightleftharpoons$ ethyl ethanoate + water

> Do not be put off by the complex appearance of the equation. It is just an example of: $A + B \rightleftharpoons C + D$

All four substances are clear, colourless liquids. They mix completely with each other.

(a) State what visible changes, if any, you would observe during the reaction.

.... **(1 mark)**

Guided (b) The reaction reaches a dynamic equilibrium after a few days.

(i) Describe what is happening to the forward and backward reactions at equilibrium.

The rate of the forward and backward reactions is ....

and they .... **(2 marks)**

(ii) State what happens to the concentrations of the reacting substances at equilibrium.

> The choices you have are: increase, decrease, do not change.

.... **(1 mark)**

Making fertilisers

1 Fertilisers may contain potassium, phosphorus and nitrogen compounds to promote plant growth.

Complete the table by placing a tick (✓) to show the elements present in the fertiliser compounds.

> What are the chemical symbols for the elements potassium, phosphorus and nitrogen?

Fertiliser compound	Element required by plants		
	Potassium	**Phosphorus**	**Nitrogen**
NH_4NO_3			✓
$(NH_4)_2SO_4$			
K_3PO_4			
KNO_3			

(3 marks)

2 Ammonium nitrate is a salt used as a fertiliser. It is made from ammonia solution and nitric acid:

ammonia + nitric acid → ammonium nitrate

Name the type of reaction that produces ammonium nitrate.

> Ammonia solution is alkaline.

.... **(1 mark)**

3 Ammonium sulfate, $(NH_4)_2SO_4$, is a salt used as a fertiliser. In the laboratory preparation of ammonium sulfate, ammonia solution is titrated with dilute sulfuric acid.

(a) Explain why titration is necessary when making a soluble salt such as ammonium sulfate from soluble reactants.

Titration lets you find the correct proportions of .... and ....

to mix together so that the solution contains only .... and .... **(2 marks)**

(b) Describe how you would produce dry crystals of ammonium sulfate from ammonium sulfate solution.

> You have to remove excess water and dry the crystals.

....

....

....

.... **(4 marks)**

4 The laboratory production of ammonium sulfate requires titration, then crystallisation. The industrial production of ammonium sulfate requires several stages. There are other differences between these ways of producing ammonium sulfate. Identify the features of each method by placing a tick (✓) in each correct box.

Feature	Laboratory	Industrial
ammonia and sulfuric acid manufactured from their raw materials		
ammonia and sulfuric acid bought from manufacturers		
small-scale production		
continuous production		

(4 marks)

Fuel cells

1 The common batteries used in torches and watches are chemical cells. Which statement about chemical cells is correct?

☐ **A** Chemical cells use a voltage until one of the reactants is used up.

☐ **B** Chemical cells produce a voltage until one of the reactants is used up.

☐ **C** Chemical cells use a voltage until all the products are used up.

☐ **D** Chemical cells produce a voltage until all the products are used up. **(1 mark)**

2 The graphs show how the potential difference (voltage) of a chemical cell and a fuel cell change during use.

Explain why the voltage of the fuel cell does not change.

A fuel cell produces a constant voltage for as long as it is supplied with

.... **(2 marks)**

3 Some electric cars use a hydrogen–oxygen fuel cell. This produces electricity for the electric motor.

(a) Name the only chemical product made by a hydrogen–oxygen fuel cell.

.... **(1 mark)**

(b) Explain why air must be supplied to the fuel cell.

> Which gas relevant to fuel cells is found in the air? What does it react with in the fuel cell?

....

.... **(2 marks)**

4 Some electric cars use a rechargeable chemical cell, rather than a hydrogen–oxygen fuel cell, to produce electricity for the electric motor. There were only four public hydrogen filling stations in the UK in 2015.

(a) Give **two** reasons why the chemical cells are likely to be more convenient for use in a car.

> Think about what happens when the car has travelled on a long journey.

1: ....

2: .... **(2 marks)**

(b) Scientists have developed a new design of hydrogen–oxygen fuel cell. Its fuel is made by the reaction of water with a stored metal hydride powder. Give one advantage of this type of fuel cell for an electric car, and give a reason for your answer.

> Think about how the fuel for a hydrogen–oxygen fuel cell is usually stored.

....

....

.... **(2 marks)**

The alkali metals

1 Compared with a typical transition metal such as iron, the alkali metals are:

☐ **A** hard with relatively low melting points

☐ **B** soft with relatively high melting points

☐ **C** soft with relatively low melting points

☐ **D** hard with relatively high melting points.   **(1 mark)**

2 Complete the table to describe the reactions of lithium, sodium and potassium with water.

Alkali metal	Flame colour	Description
lithium	does not ignite	fizzes steadily disappears slowly
sodium	orange if ignited	
potassium		

                                                                                                    (5 marks)

3 The alkali metals react with water to produce a metal hydroxide and hydrogen. For example:

> You will need an even number of hydrogen atoms on each side.

sodium + water → sodium hydroxide + hydrogen

Balance the equation for this reaction. Include state symbols.

......Na(......) + ...H_2O(......) → ......NaOH(aq) + H_2(......) .... **(2 marks)**

4 Give a reason to explain why, in terms of electronic configurations, the alkali metals occupy group 1.

> The electronic configurations of the atoms of these elements differ, but they do have something in common.

.... **(1 mark)**

5 Explain why lithium, sodium and potassium are stored in oil.

....

.... **(2 marks)**

6 Francium, Fr, is placed at the bottom of group 1.

> The group 1 hydroxides all have similar formulae.

(a) Predict the formula of francium hydroxide.

.... **(1 mark)**

(b) Predict one observation that you would expect to see in the reaction of francium with water.

.... **(1 mark)**

7 Reactivity increases going down group 1. Explain this reactivity pattern in terms of the electronic configurations of the atoms.

Going down the group, the size of the atoms ....

The outer electron becomes ....

so the outer electron is lost .... **(3 marks)**

The halogens

1 Which of the following is a chemical test for chlorine gas?

☐ **A** Damp red litmus paper turns blue, then white.

☐ **B** Damp blue litmus paper turns red, then white.

☐ **C** Damp starch–iodide paper turns red, then white.

☐ **D** Dry starch–iodide paper turns blue–black.

> **Practical skills** Answer D cannot be correct because chlorine must dissolve in water for the chemical test to work.

(1 mark)

2 Give a reason to explain why, in terms of electronic configurations, the halogens occupy group 7.

.... **(1 mark)**

Guided

3 (a) Complete the table to show the colours and physical states of the halogens at room temperature.

> You must be able to recall the colours and states of chlorine, bromine and iodine at room temperature.

Halogen	Colour	Physical state
chlorine		
bromine		
iodine	dark grey	solid (forms a purple vapour)

(4 marks)

(b) Astatine is the element placed immediately below iodine. Predict its colour and physical state.

.... **(2 marks)**

4 The table shows the densities of two halogens, in order going down group 7.

(a) Predict the density of astatine, the element placed immediately below iodine. Write its predicted density into the table. **(1 mark)**

Halogen	Density at room temperature and pressure (kg/m^3)
bromine	3103
iodine	4933
astatine	

Guided

(b) Give a reason for your answer to part (a).

> Look at the trend in density going down group 7. This should help you to make a prediction for astatine.

Going down the group, the density ....

.... **(1 mark)**

5 Fluorine, at the top of group 7, exists as simple molecules. Each molecule contains two fluorine atoms.

(a) Name the type of bond that exists between the atoms in a fluorine molecule, F_2.

> You have a choice of ionic bond, covalent bond or metallic bond.

.... **(1 mark)**

(b) Fluorine has a low boiling point. Name the type of forces or bonds that are overcome when fluorine boils.

.... **(1 mark)**

Reactions of halogens

1 Hydrogen reacts with chlorine to produce hydrogen chloride gas, HCl(g).

(a) Balance the equation for this reaction.

$$H_2(g) + Cl_2(g) \rightarrow \text{......} HCl(g)$$ **(1 mark)**

(b) What happens when hydrogen chloride gas is bubbled through water?

☐ **A** reacts vigorously, releasing oxygen   ☐ **C** dissolves to form an acidic solution

☐ **B** dissolves to form an alkaline solution   ☐ **D** dissolves to form a neutral salt solution **(1 mark)**

> **Guided**

(c) Fluorine reacts with hydrogen in the cold and dark, but chlorine and hydrogen must be exposed to sunlight in order to react. A mixture of hydrogen and bromine reacts only if a flame is put in it.

Explain what this tells you about the pattern of reactivity of the halogens.

> Look carefully at the conditions needed for hydrogen to react with the different halogens.

Going down group 7, the elements become ....

I can tell this because the energy needed for them to start reacting ....

.... **(2 marks)**

2 Sodium burns in chlorine to produce sodium chloride.

(a) Write the word equation for this reaction.

> Look at the information given to deduce the reactants and products. Do not mix words and formulae.

.... **(1 mark)**

(b) Bromine vapour reacts with hot iron wool. Red–brown iron(III) bromide, $FeBr_3$, is produced. Predict the formula of iron(III) chloride, formed in the reaction between iron and chlorine.

.... **(1 mark)**

(c) Iodine vapour reacts slowly with hot iron wool to produce grey iron(II) iodide, FeI_2.

(i) Write the formula of the iron(II) ion and the formula of the iodide ion.

> Make sure that you can recall the formulae of elements, simple compounds and ions.

iron(II) ion .... **(1 mark)**

iodide ion .... **(1 mark)**

(ii) Write the balanced equation for the reaction between iron and iodine to form iron(II) iodide.

> Remember that iodine and the other halogens exist as diatomic molecules with the general formula X_2.

.... **(2 marks)**

3 Reactivity decreases going down group 7, from fluorine to iodine. Explain, in terms of the electronic configurations of their atoms, why fluorine is more reactive than chlorine.

> **Guided**

Fluorine atoms are .... than chlorine atoms, so its outer shell is

....

and it gains an outer electron .... **(3 marks)**

Halogen displacement reactions

1 A student adds a few drops of aqueous bromine solution to a potassium iodide solution. Iodine and potassium bromide solution form.

> Answer C cannot be correct because distillation is a physical separation method, not a chemical reaction.

(a) What type of reaction is this?

☐ **A** neutralisation   ☐ **B** precipitation   ☐ **C** distillation   ☐ **D** displacement

(1 mark)

(b) Write a word equation for this reaction.

.... **(1 mark)**

2 A displacement reaction may happen when a halogen is added to a solution containing halide ions. The table shows results from an investigation with three halogens. A tick (✓) shows that displacement happens.

Halogen added	Halide ion in solution		
	Chloride	Bromide	Iodide
chlorine	not done	✓	✓
bromine	✗	not done	✓
iodine	✗	✗	not done

(a) Use the results shown in the table to deduce the order of reactivity of these halogens.

The order of reactivity, starting with the most reactive, is ....

.... because chlorine displaces ....

.... but bromine displaces only ....

Iodine .... **(3 marks)**

(b) Suggest a reason to explain why three possible experiments were not done in the investigation.

.... **(1 mark)**

(c) Explain why iodine could displace astatine from sodium astatide solution.

> Astatine is beneath iodine in group 7 of the periodic table.

....

.... **(2 marks)**

3 Fluorine is the most reactive halogen. It reacts with water to form hydrofluoric acid and oxygen.

(a) Balance the equation for the reaction between fluorine and water.

......F_2(g) + ...H_2O(l) → ......HF(aq) + O_2(g) **(1 mark)**

(b) Suggest a reason to explain why a mixture of fluorine and water cannot be used in displacement reactions.

> Look at the information given to you about fluorine and water.

.... **(1 mark)**

(c) Fluorine gas is passed over filter paper soaked in sodium chloride solution. A displacement reaction occurs but it is difficult to detect chlorine forming. Suggest a reason to explain this observation.

> Think about what you know about the appearance of chlorine.

.... **(1 mark)**

The noble gases

1 Which of these properties explains why argon is used as a shield gas during welding?

   ☐ **A** Argon is inert.   ☐ **C** Argon has a low density.

   ☐ **B** Argon is colourless.   ☐ **D** Argon is a good conductor
                                                        of electricity. **(1 mark)**

2 Explain why helium is used as a
lifting gas for party balloons
and airships.

> There are two relevant properties. For each one,
> explain why it is important for this use of helium.

Guided

Balloons and airships rise because helium ....

Helium is inert, so .... **(2 marks)**

3 The table shows some information
about the noble gases.

> Temperatures with less
> negative numbers are higher
> temperatures, so −10 °C is
> warmer than −20 °C.

Element	Melting point (°C)	Density (kg/m³)
helium	−272	0.16
neon	−248	0.41
argon	−189	0.74
krypton	−157	1.47
xenon	−111	2.21
radon	−71	3.52

   (a) Name the noble gas that has the
lowest melting point.

.... **(1 mark)**

   (b) Describe the trend in density in group 0.

.... **(1 mark)**

   (c) Oganesson, Og, was discovered early this century. It is placed in group 0 of the
periodic table, immediately below radon.
Predict the melting point of oganesson,
and explain your answer.

> What happens to the melting
> point going down group 0?

....

.... **(2 marks)**

4 The table shows the electronic
configurations of the first three noble gases.

Explain, in terms of their electronic
configurations, why these noble gases
are unreactive.

Element	Electronic configuration
helium, He	2
neon, Ne	2.8
argon, Ar	2.8.8

> Other than having two electrons in their innermost
> shells, what do these three elements have in common?

....

.... **(2 marks)**

Extended response – Groups

*The table shows the first five elements in groups 1 and 7 of the periodic table, in the order in which they are placed.

Group 1	Group 7
lithium	fluorine
sodium	chlorine
potassium	bromine
rubidium	iodine
caesium	astatine

> Sodium chloride is an ionic compound, formed when sodium forms positively charged ions and chlorine forms negatively charged ions.

When heated, sodium reacts with chlorine to produce sodium chloride:

$$2Na(s) + Cl_2(g) \rightarrow 2NaCl(s)$$

Explain, in terms of electron transfer, how sodium and chlorine react together to form sodium chloride. You may, if you wish, include diagrams to show the electronic configurations of the atoms and ions involved. Use ideas about the trends in reactivity in groups 1 and 7 to explain why the reaction between caesium and fluorine is very violent.

> What are the trends in reactivity in groups 1 and 7?

....

....

....

....

....

....

....

....

....

....

....

....

....

....

.... **(6 marks)**

> This question also covers content from Topic 1 (Key concepts in chemistry). Remember that this topic is common to Paper 1 and Paper 2, and not just covered in Paper 1.

Rates of reaction

1 Reactions happen when reactant particles collide and the collisions have sufficient energy. Complete the table by placing a tick (✓) in each correct box to explain why the rate of reaction increases.

Change in reaction conditions	Frequency of collisions increased	Energy of collisions increased
increased concentration of a reacting solution		
increased pressure of a reacting gas		
increased temperature of reaction mixture		

(3 marks)

2 Marble is mostly calcium carbonate. It reacts with dilute hydrochloric acid to produce carbon dioxide. The graph shows the results of an investigation into the effect of changing the size of marble chips on the rate of reaction with 50 cm³ of dilute hydrochloric acid. The same mass of chips, 3.2 g, was used each time.

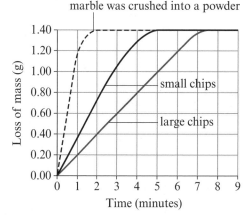

(a) State what happens to the surface area:volume ratio of a solid as the size of its particles is reduced.

.... (1 mark)

(b) Explain, in terms of the frequency of particle collisions, the expected result for powdered marble.

> Think about the surface area:volume ratio of the chips and the powder, and remember to look at the graph.

....

....

.... (2 marks)

3 (a) Describe the meaning of the term 'catalyst'.

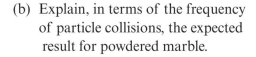

a substance that speeds up a reaction without altering the ....

and is unchanged ....

and is also unchanged.. (3 marks)

(b) Explain, in terms of activation energy, how a catalyst increases the rate of a reaction.

A catalyst provides an alternative ....

with a lower .... (2 marks)

(c) (i) State the name given to a biological catalyst. .... (1 mark)

(ii) Give one example of a commercial use of a biological catalyst.

.... (1 mark)

Investigating rates

Guided

1 Sodium thiosulfate solution and dilute hydrochloric acid are clear, colourless solutions.
They react together to form sodium chloride solution, water, sulfur dioxide and sulfur:

$$Na_2S_2O_3(aq) + 2HCl(aq) \rightarrow 2NaCl(aq) + H_2O(l) + SO_2(g) + S(s)$$

(a) Give one way in which the volume of a gas can be measured accurately.

Collect the gas in .... **(1 mark)**

(b) Sulfur dioxide is highly soluble in water. Explain why
measuring the volume of sulfur dioxide collected is **not**
an accurate way to determine the rate of this reaction.

> A *soluble* substance dissolves
> in a solvent such as water.

....

.... **(2 marks)**

(c) Suggest reasons to explain why the production
of sodium chloride solution or water **cannot**
easily be used to determine the rate of reaction.

> What changes, if any, would you
> expect to see when sodium chloride
> solution or water is produced?

....

.... **(2 marks)**

2 A student investigates how changes in the concentration
affect the rate of the reaction between $50\,cm^3$ of sodium
thiosulfate solution and $5\,cm^3$ of dilute hydrochloric
acid. The diagram shows the method that she uses.

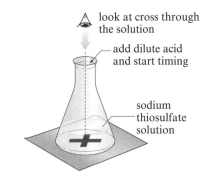

look at cross through
the solution

add dilute acid
and start timing

sodium
thiosulfate
solution

The student varies the concentration of sodium thiosulfate
solution by diluting it with water, but she uses $70\,g\,dm^{-3}$ of
hydrochloric acid each time. The table shows her results.

Concentration of $Na_2S_2O_3(aq)$ added ($g\,dm^{-3}$)	Time taken for cross on paper to disappear (s)	Relative rate of reaction, 1000/time (/s)
5	125	
15	42	24
25	25	

view through solution

time

As time goes on, the solution gets more cloudy.
The cross 'disappears'.

(a) State **two** steps that the student takes to obtain
valid results.

> Think about the variables, other than the
> concentration of sodium thiosulfate.

1: ....

2: .... **(2 marks)**

(b) Complete the table to show the
relative rate of each reaction.

Guided

> 🖩 **Maths skills** Use a calculator to calculate
> $1000 \div$ time for $5\,g\,dm^{-3}$ and
> $25\,g\,dm^{-3}$ of $Na_2S_2O_3(aq)$.

(2 marks)

(c) Describe what happens to the relative
rate of reaction as the concentration of
the sodium thiosulfate solution increases.

....

.... **(2 marks)**

Exam skills – Rates of reaction

1 Calcium carbonate reacts with dilute hydrochloric acid:

calcium carbonate + hydrochloric acid →
calcium chloride + water + carbon dioxide

A student adds lumps of calcium carbonate to an excess of dilute hydrochloric acid in a flask. He measures the change in mass that happens as carbon dioxide gas escapes from the flask. The table shows his results.

Time (s)	Change in mass (g)
0	0.00
20	0.48
40	0.76
60	0.88
80	0.94
100	0.96
120	0.96

(a) Plot a graph of change in mass against time using the grid.

(3 marks)

> Use × or + for each point, and draw a single line of best fit. The line does not have to be a straight line.

> **Maths skills** Aim to plot each point to within half a square of its accurate position, or better.

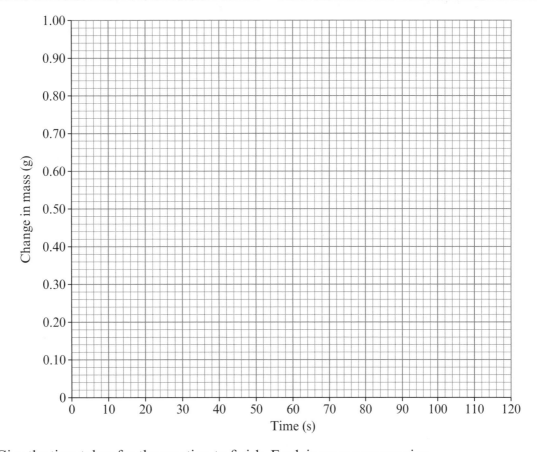

(b) Give the time taken for the reaction to finish. Explain your answer using information from the table or your graph.

Time taken: ....

Explanation: ....

.... **(2 marks)**

(c) The student repeats the experiment. He keeps all the conditions the same, but increases the temperature of the dilute hydrochloric acid. On the grid, sketch a line that the student should obtain for this experiment. Label this line **C**.

> You do not need to plot individual points for this line.

(2 marks)

Heat energy changes

1   Describe, in terms of energy transfers, the difference between an exothermic process and an endothermic process.

> Guided

> Think about whether heat energy is taken in or given out in these processes.

In an exothermic change or reaction, heat energy is ....

but, in an endothermic change or reaction, heat energy is .... **(2 marks)**

2   Breaking bonds and making bonds involves energy transfers. Which row (**A**, **B**, **C** or **D**) in the table correctly describes these processes?

> Answer A cannot be correct because one process is endothermic and the other is exothermic.

	Bond breaking	Bond making
☐ A	exothermic	exothermic
☐ B	exothermic	endothermic
☐ C	endothermic	exothermic
☐ D	endothermic	endothermic

(1 mark)

3   Changes in heat energy occur when salts dissolve in water.

(a) Ammonium nitrate is dissolved in water. The temperature of the reaction mixture decreases.

State whether this process is exothermic or endothermic.

.... **(1 mark)**

(b) Give one type of reaction, which takes place in aqueous solution, that is always exothermic.

> Reactions that happen in solution include precipitation, neutralisation and displacement reactions.

.... **(1 mark)**

4   Magnesium reacts with dilute hydrochloric acid, forming magnesium chloride solution and hydrogen gas.

(a) Describe the measurements that you would take to confirm that the reaction is exothermic.

> **Practical skills** Outline what you would measure, the measuring apparatus and how you would use the results.

....

....

.... **(3 marks)**

(b) Balance the equation for this reaction, and include state symbols.

$Mg(......) + ...HCl(......) \rightarrow MgCl_2(......) + H_2(......)$ **(2 marks)**

> Guided

(c) Explain, in terms of breaking bonds and making bonds, why this reaction is exothermic.

> Mention heat energy in your answer.

More ....

is released when bonds ....

than is needed to .... **(3 marks)**

Reaction profiles

1 Give the term used to describe the minimum energy needed to start a reaction.

.... **(1 mark)**

2 Methane burns completely in oxygen to form carbon dioxide and water vapour:

$$CH_4(g) + 2O_2(g) \rightarrow CO_2(g) + 2H_2O(g)$$

reactants   products

The diagram shows a simple reaction profile for this reaction.

Explain, using information in the diagram, how you can tell that this reaction is exothermic.

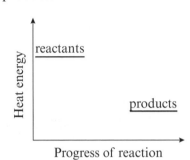

> Is heat energy given out or taken in during this reaction?

There is more stored energy in the ....

than in the ....

so, during the reaction, energy is .... **(2 marks)**

3 Carbon burns completely in excess oxygen to form carbon dioxide: $C(s) + O_2(g) \rightarrow CO_2(g)$

Complete the reaction profile for this reaction by showing the activation energy.

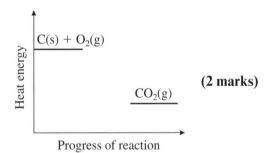

(2 marks)

> You will need to draw a curved line between the reactant and product lines, and add a labelled arrow.

4 Calcium carbonate decomposes when heated strongly, forming calcium oxide and carbon dioxide:

$$CaCO_3(s) \rightarrow CaO(s) + CO_2(g)$$

The reaction is endothermic.

Label the reaction profile diagram to show the overall energy change and the activation energy.

> You will need to draw at least one dashed line and two labelled arrows.

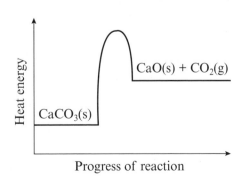

(2 marks)

Crude oil

1 (a) How long does it take for crude oil to form?

  ☐ **A** tens of years   ☐ **C** thousands of years

  ☐ **B** hundreds of years   ☐ **D** millions of years   **(1 mark)**

(b) Crude oil is described as mainly a complex mixture of:

  ☐ **A** hydrogen and carbon   ☐ **C** polymers

  ☐ **B** alkenes   ☐ **D** hydrocarbons   **(1 mark)**

(c) Crude oil is a **finite** resource. Explain what this means.

> Use the correct answer to part **(a)** to help you.

....

.... **(1 mark)**

2 The diagrams show the structure of two compounds, hexane and cyclohexane.

hexane

cyclohexane

(a) The molecular formula of hexane is C_6H_{14}. Give the molecular formula of cyclohexane.

> Count the numbers of atoms of each element in the diagram of cyclohexane.

.... **(1 mark)**

Guided

(b) Explain why hexane and cyclohexane are hydrocarbons.

They are compounds of ....

.... **(2 marks)**

3 Crude oil is an important source of fuels.

(a) Give one example of a fuel obtained from crude oil.

.... **(1 mark)**

(b) Petrochemicals are substances made from crude oil. They include polymers such as poly(ethene). Crude oil is a feedstock for the petrochemical industry. Explain the meaning of the term '**feedstock**'.

....

....

.... **(2 marks)**

Fractional distillation

1   Crude oil is separated into simpler, more useful mixtures by fractional distillation. The diagram shows the main fractions obtained from crude oil.

crude oil →

→ gases
→ petrol
→ kerosene
→ diesel oil
→ fuel oil
→ bitumen

(a)   Name the oil fraction that:

(i)   has the smallest number of carbon atoms and hydrogen atoms in its molecules

.... **(1 mark)**

(ii)   contains substances with the highest boiling points

.... **(1 mark)**

(iii)   is easiest to ignite

.... **(1 mark)**

(iv)   has the highest viscosity.

> Viscosity is a measure of how difficult it is for a substance to flow.

.... **(1 mark)**

(b)   Name the oil fraction that is used:

(i)   to surface roads and roofs

.... **(1 mark)**

(ii)   as a fuel for aircraft.

.... **(1 mark)**

(c)   Name two oil fractions that are used as fuels for cars.

.... **(2 marks)**

2   Most of the hydrocarbons in crude oil are members of a particular homologous series. Name this series.

.... **(1 mark)**

3   Describe how crude oil is separated using fractional distillation.

Guided

Oil is heated so that it ....

The vapours are passed into a column, which is hot at the ....

and cold at the .... Hydrocarbons rise, and ....

at different heights, depending on .... **(4 marks)**

Alkanes

1   Natural gas is a hydrocarbon fuel. It is mainly methane, CH_4. Which of the following substances **cannot** be produced when methane burns in air?

☐ **A** water   ☐ **B** carbon   ☐ **C** hydrogen   ☐ **D** carbon dioxide   **(1 mark)**

2   Which row correctly shows two features of a homologous series?

	Physical properties	**Chemical properties**
☐ **A**	show a gradual variation	are similar
☐ **B**	show a gradual variation	show a gradual variation
☐ **C**	are similar	show a gradual variation
☐ **D**	are similar	are similar

> Physical properties include melting points and boiling points.

(1 mark)

3   The alkanes form a homologous series of hydrocarbons. The diagrams show the structures of the first two alkanes, methane and ethane.

```
      H                          H   H
      |                          |   |
  H—C—H                     H—C—C—H
      |                          |   |
      H                          H   H
   methane                      ethane
```

(a) Write the molecular formula of ethane.

> The molecular formula of methane is shown in question 1, and the structures of methane and ethane above.

.... **(1 mark)**

(b) The next alkane in the homologous series is propane, C_3H_8. Draw the structure of propane, showing all the covalent bonds.

> Show each covalent bond as a straight line.

(1 mark)

Guided

(c) Deduce how the molecular formula of an alkane differs from its neighbouring compounds.

> Compare the three molecular formulae. It may also help to compare the three structures.

Going from one alkane to the next, the molecular formula changes by ....

.... **(1 mark)**

4   (a) State the general formula for the alkanes.

> What pattern is shown by the molecular formulae for methane in question 1, and for ethane and propane in question 3?

Guided

C_nH .... **(1 mark)**

(b) Predict the molecular formula for hexane, an alkane that has six carbon atoms in its molecules.

.... **(1 mark)**

Incomplete combustion

1 Petrol is a hydrocarbon fuel. When it burns in air, waste products form and energy is transferred to the surroundings.

(a) Which releases the most energy from $1\,dm^3$ of petrol: complete combustion or incomplete combustion?

.... **(1 mark)**

> **Guided**

(b) Complete the table by placing a tick (✓) in each correct box to show the products formed in each type of combustion.

	Incomplete combustion	Complete combustion
Water		✓
Carbon		
Carbon monoxide		
Carbon dioxide	✓	

(2 marks)

2 Diagrams **A** and **B** show two flames produced by a Bunsen burner. The air hole is closed in diagram **A** but open in diagram **B**. If the air hole is closed, less oxygen can enter the chimney to mix with the natural gas.

Explain which flame (**A** or **B**) will coat the bottom of a gauze mat with a black substance.

....

....

.... **(2 marks)**

3 The combustion of diesel oil can produce carbon particles and carbon monoxide gas.

(a) Give a reason to explain why carbon particles may be harmful to health if breathed in.

.... **(1 mark)**

(b) Balance the equation below, which models a combustion reaction of benzene (a liquid hydrocarbon).

> First balance the number of water molecules needed, then the number of oxygen molecules needed.

$C_6H_6 +$ ......$O_2 \rightarrow 2C + 3CO + CO_2 +$ ......H_2O **(1 mark)**

> **Guided**

(c) Explain why carbon monoxide is toxic.

When breathed in, carbon monoxide combines with ....

so .... **(2 marks)**

Acid rain

Guided

1 (a) Complete the diagram below using labels from the box.

| acid rain | power station | rain cloud | acidic gases | distant city |

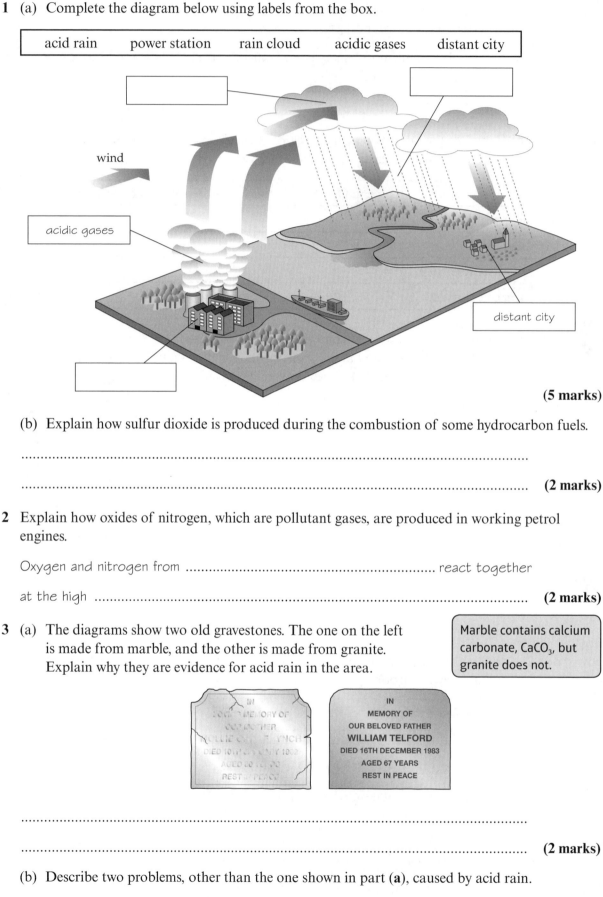

wind

acidic gases

distant city

(5 marks)

(b) Explain how sulfur dioxide is produced during the combustion of some hydrocarbon fuels.

....

.... **(2 marks)**

Guided

2 Explain how oxides of nitrogen, which are pollutant gases, are produced in working petrol engines.

Oxygen and nitrogen from .... react together

at the high .... **(2 marks)**

3 (a) The diagrams show two old gravestones. The one on the left is made from marble, and the other is made from granite. Explain why they are evidence for acid rain in the area.

> Marble contains calcium carbonate, $CaCO_3$, but granite does not.

IN
LOVING MEMORY OF
OUR MOTHER
MOLLIE O... Y LYNCH
DIED 10TH ... JY 1982
AGED 80 ... RS
REST ... PEACE

IN
MEMORY OF
OUR BELOVED FATHER
WILLIAM TELFORD
DIED 16TH DECEMBER 1983
AGED 67 YEARS
REST IN PEACE

....

.... **(2 marks)**

(b) Describe two problems, other than the one shown in part (**a**), caused by acid rain.

....

.... **(2 marks)**

Choosing fuels

1 Petrol, kerosene and diesel oil are fossil fuels.

(a) State the name of the substance from which these fuels are obtained.

.... **(1 mark)**

(b) Give one example of how each fuel is used.

Petrol is used as a fuel for cars. Kerosene is used as a ....

and diesel oil is used .... **(2 marks)**

2 Crude oil and natural gas are finite resources because they take a very long time to form, or are no longer being made. Methane is a non-renewable fossil fuel that is found in natural gas.

> Non-renewable and finite have different meanings. Do not answer by writing 'it is not renewable'.

State why methane is described as **non-renewable**.

.... **(1 mark)**

3 Hydrogen and petrol may both be used as fuels for cars.

(a) Complete the balanced equation for the reaction between hydrogen and oxygen.

> There is only one product.

$2H_2 + O_2 \rightarrow$ .... **(1 mark)**

(b) Petrol is a complex mixture of hydrocarbons. Name one product of the **complete combustion** of petrol that is **not** produced when hydrogen burns.

.... **(1 mark)**

4 The table shows some information about hydrogen gas and liquid petrol.

Fuel	Energy released by 1 dm³ of fuel (MJ)	Energy released by 1 kg of fuel (MJ)
hydrogen	0.012	142
petrol	35	47

(a) Using information from the table, identify an advantage of using:

(i) petrol rather than hydrogen as a fuel for cars

.... **(1 mark)**

(ii) hydrogen rather than petrol as a fuel for cars.

.... **(1 mark)**

(b) Suggest a reason to explain why there is an advantage to storing hydrogen in car fuel tanks as a liquid, rather than as a gas.

> Think about the closeness of particles in liquids and gases.

....

.... **(1 mark)**

Cracking

1 In the diagram below, a cracking reaction is modelled using the structures of the molecules.

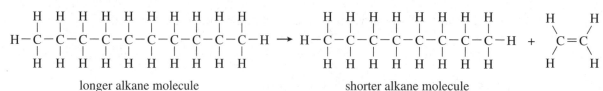

longer alkane molecule   shorter alkane molecule

(a) Name the **type** of hydrocarbon shown by the smallest molecule above.

.... **(1 mark)**

> **Guided**

(b) Write the balanced equation, using molecular formulae, for this cracking reaction.

> Count the carbon atoms and hydrogen atoms in each molecule to work out the formulae needed.

$C_{10}H$ .... **(2 marks)**

2 Alkanes and alkenes form two different homologous series. Which row in the table correctly describes each type of hydrocarbon?

	Alkanes	Alkenes
☐ A	saturated	contain only C–H and C–C bonds
☐ B	unsaturated	contain only C–H and C–C bonds
☐ C	contain only C–H and C–C bonds	saturated
☐ D	contain only C–H and C–C bonds	unsaturated

(1 mark)

3 The apparatus shown in the diagram can be used to crack the alkanes in liquid paraffin.

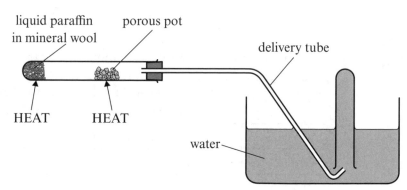

liquid paraffin in mineral wool   porous pot   delivery tube

HEAT   HEAT

water

(a) State the purpose of the porous pot.

.... **(1 mark)**

> **Guided**

(b) Explain what is meant by **cracking**.

a reaction in which larger alkanes are broken down into ....

....

.... **(2 marks)**

4 Crude oil is separated into more useful mixtures called fractions by fractional distillation. Give **two** reasons why an oil refinery may crack the fractions containing larger alkanes.

> **Guided**

Smaller hydrocarbons are ....

Cracking helps to match .... **(2 marks)**

Extended response – Fuels

*Camping gas is a mixture of propane and butane, obtained from crude oil. It is a rainy day and some campers are making tea inside their tent. Incomplete combustion of the camping gas could occur if the campers do not take adequate precautions.

> How does incomplete combustion occur?

Explain how incomplete combustion of hydrocarbons such as propane and butane occurs, and the problems that it can cause in a situation similar to this one. You may include a balanced equation in your answer.

> Which is a more efficient use of fuels, complete or incomplete combustion, and why does this matter?

> What are the products of the incomplete combustion of hydrocarbons? What problems do they cause?

....

....

....

....

....

....

....

....

....

....

....

....

....

....

.... **(6 marks)**

> Carbon dioxide may be produced during incomplete combustion as well as during complete combustion, and so does not explain the problems that this gas causes.

The early atmosphere

1 The gases that formed the Earth's earliest atmosphere are thought to have come from:

☐ **A** combustion

☐ **B** volcanic activity

☐ **C** photosynthesis

☐ **D** condensation   **(1 mark)**

2 The pie chart shows the possible percentages of three gases in the Earth's early atmosphere.

Key
■ carbon dioxide
■ water vapour
☐ other gases

10%

80%

Maths skills Use the key to identify the sector that represents carbon dioxide.

(a) State the percentage of carbon dioxide in the early atmosphere, as shown by this pie chart.

....   **(1 mark)**

(b) Explain how oceans formed as the early Earth cooled.

....

....   **(2 marks)**

(c) The Earth's atmosphere today contains about 0.04% carbon dioxide. Explain how the oceans contributed to the decrease in the percentage of carbon dioxide in the atmosphere.

Think about whether carbon dioxide is soluble or insoluble in water.

....

....   **(2 marks)**

3 The Earth's atmosphere today contains more oxygen than its early atmosphere did.

Write down what you would do and what you would observe.

(a) Describe the chemical test for oxygen.

....

....   **(2 marks)**

> **Guided** (b) Explain why the percentage of oxygen in the atmosphere has gradually increased.

In your answer, include the name of the process involved.

The growth of primitive plants used ....

and released ....

by the process of ....   **(3 marks)**

Greenhouse effect

1   Which of these gases are both greenhouse gases?

   ☐ **A**   oxygen and carbon dioxide

   ☐ **B**   carbon dioxide and water vapour

   ☐ **C**   nitrogen and carbon dioxide

   ☐ **D**   oxygen and nitrogen

   (1 mark)

2   The table shows processes involved in the greenhouse effect. Add a number to each box to order the processes from **1** (first) to **4** (last).

Process	Order (1–4)
Gases in the atmosphere absorb heat radiated from the Earth.	
Released energy keeps the Earth warm.	4
Heat is radiated from the Earth's surface.	
Gases in the atmosphere release energy in random directions.	

   (3 marks)

3   Carbon dioxide is described as a greenhouse gas.

   (a) Name another greenhouse gas, often released as a result of livestock farming.

   ....   **(1 mark)**

   (b) Explain why the use of fossil fuels causes the release of carbon dioxide.

   > What type of substance is found in fossil fuels such as petrol? What happens when they are burned?

   ....

   ....   **(2 marks)**

4   The graphs show how the mean global temperature and the percentage of carbon dioxide in the atmosphere have changed over the last 220 000 years.

   — difference in temperature

   ▆ percentage of CO_2 in the air

   200   1850   100   50   0
   Thousands of years before today

   (a) State what happens, in general, to the mean global temperature as the percentage of carbon dioxide in the air increases.

   ....   **(1 mark)**

   (b) State what is meant by **global warming**.

   > Do not use the words **global** or **warming** in your answer.

   a worldwide ....   **(1 mark)**

   (c) State **two** environmental effects of global warming.

   1: ....   **(1 mark)**

   2: ....   **(1 mark)**

Extended response – Atmospheric science

*The graphs show the change in mean global temperature, and the concentration of carbon dioxide in the atmosphere, between the years 1850 and 2005.

> A higher temperature than the mean temperature gives a positive temperature change on the graph.

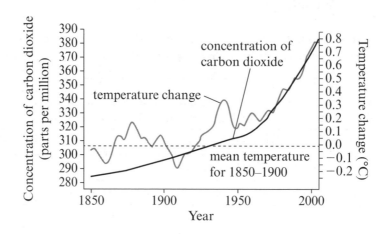

Evaluate whether these graphs provide evidence that human activity is causing the Earth's temperature to increase. In your answer, explain how carbon dioxide acts as a greenhouse gas, and describe processes that release carbon dioxide or remove it from the atmosphere.

....

....

....

....

....

....

....

....

....

....

....

....

.... **(6 marks)**

> You should be able to evaluate evidence for human activity causing climate change. This could include correlations between the change in atmospheric carbon dioxide concentration, the consumption of fossil fuels and temperature change.

Tests for metal ions

1 Some metal ions in compounds can be identified using flame tests. Draw a straight line to match each metal ion to its correct flame test colour.

Metal ion	Flame test colour
calcium, Ca^{2+} •	• red
copper, Cu^{2+} •	• yellow
lithium, Li^+ •	• lilac
potassium, K^+ •	• orange–red
sodium, Na^+ •	• blue–green

(4 marks)

2 A student carries out a flame test on a sample of sodium chloride. This is the method that she uses:

> **Method**
>
> - Open the Bunsen burner air hole half-way to get a flame that is neither luminous nor roaring.
> - Dip a clean wire loop into hydrochloric acid, and then into the sample.
> - Put the tip of the wire loop into the edge of the flame and record the flame colour.

(a) Suggest a reason to explain why the flame test loop must be clean before carrying out the test.

.... **(1 mark)**

(b) Suggest a reason to explain why the flame must not be a luminous flame.

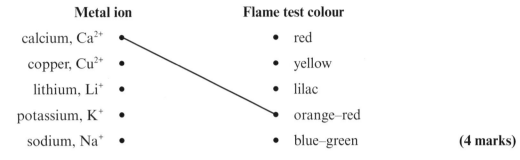

A luminous flame is the orange 'safety' flame.

.... **(1 mark)**

3 Different metal ions produce different coloured metal hydroxide precipitates.

(a) A student adds a few drops of sodium hydroxide solution to a sample of copper chloride solution. State the colour of the precipitate formed in the test.

.... **(1 mark)**

(b) Describe how you would distinguish between iron(II) sulfate solution and iron(III) sulfate solution using this test.

You do not need to describe the test, only the colours of the precipitates formed with each solution.

....

.... **(2 marks)**

(c) Calcium hydroxide and aluminium hydroxide are both white. Describe how you would distinguish between them using more sodium hydroxide solution.

I would add more sodium hydroxide solution to the white precipitate.

Aluminium hydroxide ....

but calcium hydroxide .... **(2 marks)**

More tests for ions

1 Some halide ions can be identified using silver nitrate solution. Different coloured silver halide precipitates form.

(a) Draw a straight line to match each halide ion to its silver halide precipitate colour.

Halide ion	Silver halide precipitate colour
bromide, Br^- •	• white
chloride, Cl^- •	• cream
iodide, I^- •	• yellow

(3 marks)

Guided

(b) The sample is acidified using dilute nitric acid. Explain why the sample should **not** be acidified using dilute hydrochloric acid.

Hydrochloric acid contains .... ions, which would react

with silver ions to form a white .... **(2 marks)**

2 Carbonate ions, CO_3^{2-}, present in a sample can be identified by adding dilute acid.

(a) State the observation expected in this test.

.... **(1 mark)**

(b) Describe a test to confirm the results seen in your answer to part (a).

> Describe the chemical test for carbon dioxide – write down what you would do and what you would see.

....

.... **(2 marks)**

3 Sulfate ions, SO_4^{2-}, present in a sample can be identified by adding barium chloride solution.

(a) Name the white precipitate formed in this test.

.... **(1 mark)**

Guided

(b) Explain why the sample must be acidified with dilute hydrochloric acid for this test.

> **Practical skills** Barium carbonate is a white, insoluble solid.

The hydrochloric acid reacts with any .... ions,

so they cannot .... **(2 marks)**

4 Ammonium ions, NH_4^+, can be identified by adding dilute sodium hydroxide solution to the sample and then warming the mixture.

(a) Name the gas produced in this test.

.... **(1 mark)**

Guided

(b) Describe the chemical test for the gas produced in this test.

Damp .... litmus paper turns .... **(2 marks)**

Instrumental methods

1 Flame photometry is an instrumental method of chemical analysis. Several different instrumental methods are available. Describe **two** ways in which they improve chemical tests.

1: ....

2: .... **(2 marks)**

2 The emission spectra below were produced by flame photometry.

(a) The mix that produces the bottom spectrum contains two different metal ions.

(i) Explain how you can tell that the mix does **not** contain lithium ions.

Compare the lines in the spectrum for lithium ions with those in the spectrum for the mix. Are any of them the same?

Li$^+$
Na$^+$
K$^+$
Ca^{2+}
Cu^{2+}
mix

....

....

.... **(2 marks)**

(ii) Identify the formulae of the ions present in the mix.

Look at the lines in the spectrum for the mix. Which other spectra also show these lines?

1: ....

2: .... **(2 marks)**

⟩ **Guided** ⟩ (b) Describe how you could use emission spectra to identify an ion in an unknown solution.

Obtain the reference spectra for different ions, then compare them with

the spectrum from ....

If the lines .... **(2 marks)**

3 Data from the flame photometer can be used to determine the concentration of ions in dilute solution. The diagram shows a calibration curve for potassium ions in solution.

(a) Deduce the concentration of potassium ions that gives a reading of 20%.

Photometer reading (%)

Concentration of potassium ions (g dm^{-3})

.... g dm^{-3} **(1 mark)**

(b) Deduce the reading obtained using a solution containing 0.27 g dm^{-3} of potassium ions.

.... % **(1 mark)**

 **Practical skills**

Extended response – Tests for ions

*The labels have come off four storage bottles:

ammonium sulfate	lithium carbonate	sodium sulfate	aluminium sulfate
$(NH_4)_2SO_4$	Li_2CO_3	Na_2SO_4	$Al_2(SO_4)_3$

Each bottle contains a different white crystalline solid.
Each solid is soluble in water.

> If each solid is soluble in water, you could carry out tests on each solid or its solution as appropriate.

Explain how, using simple chemical tests, you could identify which substance each bottle contains.

> There are several possible sequences of tests to distinguish between the substances. Depending on your choice, you may not need to mention all the tests in your answer.

....

....

....

....

....

....

....

....

....

....

....

....

....

....

....

....

....   **(6 marks)**

> You should be able to identify the ions in unknown salts using any of the chemical tests in the specification.

More about alkanes

1 Pentane, C_5H_{12}, is an alkane found in petrol. It undergoes complete combustion in excess oxygen.

(a) Name the products formed by the complete combustion of pentane.

.... **(2 marks)**

(b) Balance the equation for the complete combustion of pentane.

> Balance the number of H_2O molecules first, then the number of CO_2 molecules. Finally, balance the number of oxygen molecules.

$C_5H_{12} + ... O_2 \rightarrow ......CO_2 + ...H_2O$ **(1 mark)**

(c) Diesel oil contains hexadecane, an alkane with 16 carbon atoms in its molecules. Deduce its molecular formula.

> The general formula for alkanes is C_nH_{2n+2}.

.... **(1 mark)**

2 The diagram shows the structure of a molecule of propane.

Propane is a saturated hydrocarbon.

(a) Explain why propane is a hydrocarbon.

> Is propane a mixture or a compound? Which elements does it contain?

....

.... **(2 marks)**

> Guided

(b) Explain why propane is described as **saturated**.

Propane does not contain .... ;

it contains only .... **(2 marks)**

> Guided

3 The table shows some information about some alkanes. Complete the table.

> You must be able to recall the formulae of the first four alkanes, and draw the structures of their molecules.

Name of alkane	Molecular formula	Structure
methane		(H–C–H structure with H above and below)
ethane		(H₃C–CH₃ structure)
butane	C_4H_{10}	

(3 marks)

Alkenes

1 The diagram shows the structure of a molecule of ethene.

(a) Explain why ethene is described as an unsaturated hydrocarbon.

$$\begin{array}{cc} H & H \\ \diagdown & \diagup \\ C = C \\ \diagup & \diagdown \\ H & H \end{array}$$

It is a hydrocarbon because it is a compound of ....

....

It is unsaturated because it contains .... bonds.   **(3 marks)**

(b) Balance the equation for the complete combustion of ethene.

> Balance the number of water molecules first, then the number of carbon dioxide molecules. Finally, balance the number of oxygen molecules.

$C_2H_4 + ...O_2 \rightarrow ......CO_2 + ...H_2O$ **(1 mark)**

(c) Decene is an alkene with 10 carbon atoms in its molecules. Deduce its molecular formula.

> The general formula for alkenes is C_nH_{2n}.

....   **(1 mark)**

2 Alkenes undergo addition reactions with bromine water.

Describe a chemical test to distinguish between the liquids hexane and hexene.

> Write down what you would do and what you would observe for hexane and for hexene.

....

....

....   **(2 marks)**

3 The table shows some information about some alkenes. Complete the table.

Name of alkene	Molecular formula	Structure
propene	C_3H_6	
butene		$\begin{array}{c} H \quad H \qquad\quad H \\ | \quad | \qquad\quad \diagup \\ H-C-C-C=C \\ | \quad | \quad | \quad\, \diagdown \\ H \quad H \quad H \quad H \end{array}$

(2 marks)

> You can draw all the bond angles at 90° if you find this easier.
>
> You must be able to recall the formulae of the first three alkenes, and draw the structures of their molecules.

Addition polymers

1 Poly(chloroethene), also called PVC, is used as a component of household electrical cables. Which pair of properties does PVC have that make it suitable for this use?

☐ **A** good electrical conductor and rigid

☐ **B** poor electrical conductor and rigid

☐ **C** poor electrical conductor and flexible

☐ **D** good electrical conductor and flexible   **(1 mark)**

2 State the meaning of the term '**polymer**'.

a substance of high average ....

made up of small .... **(2 marks)**

3 Ethene molecules, C_2H_4, can combine in a polymerisation reaction.

(a) Name the polymer formed in the reaction.

.... **(1 mark)**

(b) State the feature of ethene molecules that allows them to take part in this reaction.

.... **(1 mark)**

(c) State the type of polymerisation reaction involved.

.... **(1 mark)**

4 The diagram shows the repeating unit of a polymer.

$$\left[\begin{array}{cc} H & H \\ | & | \\ C & C \\ | & | \\ H & CH_3 \end{array}\right]$$

Draw the structure of a molecule of the monomer that was used to produce this polymer.

> Your diagram should contain a C=C bond and no brackets. Remember that carbon atoms form four bonds.

(1 mark)

5 The diagram shows the structure of a molecule of tetrafluoroethene, C_2F_4.

$$\begin{array}{ccc} F & & F \\ \diagdown & & \diagup \\ & C=C & \\ \diagup & & \diagdown \\ F & & F \end{array}$$

Draw the structure of poly(tetrafluoroethene), the polymer that forms from this substance.

> You only need to draw the structure of the repeating unit. Your diagram should not contain a C=C bond, but it should have brackets, as in the diagram shown in question 4.

(1 mark)

Biological polymers

1 DNA, deoxyribonucleic acid, is a biological polymer. It is found in the nucleus of cells.

(a) State the number of **different** monomers found in a DNA molecule.

   ....   **(1 mark)**

(b) Give the name of the type of
    monomers that produce a DNA molecule.

> You are **not** being asked to name each different monomer.

   ....   **(1 mark)**

2 Proteins are biological polymers.
   There are many different types of proteins in living organisms.

(a) Give the name of the monomers that produce a protein molecule.

   ....   **(1 mark)**

(b) The diagram shows the structure of glycine, which is an
    example of the type of monomer that produces proteins.

$$
\begin{array}{ccccc}
H & & H & & O \\
\diagdown & & | & & \diagup\!\!\diagup \\
 & N-&C-&C & \\
\diagup & & | & & \diagdown \\
H & & H & & O-H
\end{array}
$$

   Give the molecular formula of glycine.

> Count the numbers of atoms of each element in a glycine molecule.

   ....   **(1 mark)**

3 Starch is a biological polymer made when
   glucose monomers react together.

(a) The molecular formula of glucose is $C_6H_{12}O_6$.
    Deduce the empirical formula of glucose.

> This is the simplest whole number ratio of the atoms of each element in the compound.

   ....   **(1 mark)**

> **Guided**

(b) Describe why glucose is an example of a **carbohydrate**.

> The ending '-ate' shows that oxygen is one of the elements present. It also contains two other elements.

   It contains atoms of ....   **(1 mark)**

(c) Other than a carbohydrate, state the type of
    substances to which glucose belongs.

> Many of these taste sweet.

   ....   **(1 mark)**

Polymer problems

1 There are problems associated with the disposal of polymers. Draw a straight line to match each disposal method to its typical problem.

Disposal method	Typical problem
combustion •	• suitable sites running out
burial in landfill •	• harmful gases produced
break down by microbes •	• different polymers must be sorted
recycling •	• many polymers are non-biodegradable **(4 marks)**

2 Landfill sites are used to dispose of many waste materials, including polymers.

> State what it is, and outline what happens to the waste materials that are brought to it.

(a) Describe what a landfill site is.

....

.... **(2 marks)**

> **Guided**

(b) Describe one problem caused by non-biodegradable polymers in landfill sites.

The polymers do not decompose, so the landfill sites ....

.... **(1 mark)**

3 Polymers may be disposed of by incineration (combustion at very high temperatures).

(a) The complete combustion of poly(ethene) produces carbon dioxide and water.

(i) Write the word equation for this reaction.

.... **(1 mark)**

(ii) State one environmental problem caused by increasing concentrations of carbon dioxide in the atmosphere.

.... **(1 mark)**

(b) Describe **two** advantages of using incineration rather than landfill sites to dispose of waste polymers.

> What happens to the volume of waste left over after each method of disposal?

1: ....

2: .... **(2 marks)**

4 Different polymers have different properties. Household items may be made from different polymers. For example, shampoo bottles often have a clear container with a coloured lid made from a different polymer.

> Look again at the information in the stem of the question.

(a) Give a disadvantage of recycling polymers.

.... **(1 mark)**

(b) Crude oil is the raw material for making most polymers. Explain an advantage of recycling polymers.

> Crude oil is a finite resource.

....

.... **(2 marks)**

Extended response – Hydrocarbons and polymers

*The diagram shows the structure of ethene.

$$H \quad \quad H$$
$$\diagdown \quad \diagup$$
$$C = C$$
$$\diagup \quad \diagdown$$
$$H \quad \quad H$$

DNA, starch and proteins are naturally occurring polymers made from other substances. Poly(ethene) is an artificial polymer made from ethene.

State the monomers needed to make each type of naturally occurring polymer. Explain how ethene forms poly(ethene). You should include the type of polymerisation that produces poly(ethene), and an equation to show its formation.

> The equation should show the structures of ethene and poly(ethene).

....

....

....

....

....

....

....

....

....

....

....

....

....

....

....

....

....

.... **(6 marks)**

> You should be prepared to describe how other artificial polymers can be made, including poly(propene), poly(chloroethene) and poly(tetrafluoroethene).

Alcohols

1 Ethanol, C_2H_5OH, is an alcohol. It can be converted into ethanoic acid, CH_3COOH, by the action of microbes. What happens to the ethanol in this reaction?

> Answer D cannot be correct because solutions of alcohols are neither acidic nor alkaline.

   ☐ **A** It is oxidised.   ☐ **C** It is dehydrated.

   ☐ **B** It is reduced.   ☐ **D** It is neutralised.   **(1 mark)**

Guided

2 The table shows some information about some alcohols.

Name of alcohol	Formula	Structure
methanol		H—C—O—H (with H above and H below the C)
ethanol	C_2H_5OH	
propanol	C_3H_7OH	H—C—C—C—O—H (with H above and H below each C)

(a) Complete the table.

> Show all the covalent bonds in your structure.

      (2 marks)

(b) Identify the functional group in alcohols by drawing a circle around it in the structure for propanol.   **(1 mark)**

(c) Give **two** reasons why these three compounds belong to the same homologous series.

> Look at the similarities and differences in their formulae and structures.

     1: ....

     2: ....   **(2 marks)**

3 Ethanol reacts with sodium to produce hydrogen and a soluble salt called sodium ethoxide:

     $2C_2H_5OH(l) + 2Na(s) \rightarrow H_2(g) + 2C_2H_5ONa(aq)$

> Look at the state symbols in the balanced equation.

(a) Predict **two** observations that you would see in this reaction.

     1: ....

     2: ....   **(2 marks)**

(b) Describe a chemical test that you could use to show that sodium ethoxide solution is alkaline.

> State what you would do and what you would observe.

....

....   **(2 marks)**

(c) Balance the equation for the complete combustion of ethanol.

     $C_2H_5OH + ...O_2 \rightarrow ......CO_2 + ...H_2O$ **(1 mark)**

Making ethanol

1 Ethanol can be made from carbohydrates by fermentation under anaerobic conditions.

(a) What other product is made during fermentation?

☐ **A** oxygen   ☐ **C** carbon dioxide

☐ **B** hydrogen   ☐ **D** water vapour   **(1 mark)**

(b) Which of these temperatures is most suitable for fermentation?

☐ **A** 5°C   ☐ **C** 65°C

☐ **B** 35°C   ☐ **D** 75°C   **(1 mark)**

(c) Name the type of soluble carbohydrate used in fermentation.

.... **(1 mark)**

(d) State why yeast is needed for fermentation to happen. | The yeast is not a reactant in fermentation. |

.... **(1 mark)**

(e) Describe what is meant by anaerobic conditions. | The word *aerobic* is to do with oxygen. |

.... **(1 mark)**

2 Fractional distillation is used to obtain a concentrated solution of ethanol from a fermentation mixture.

(a) State the physical property that allows ethanol to be separated from water by fractional distillation.

.... **(1 mark)**

Guided (b) The diagram shows the apparatus used for the fractional distillation of ethanol.

Describe how this apparatus is used to obtain a concentrated solution of ethanol.

Heat the dilute solution of ethanol using ....

Ethanol has a lower .... than water so it ....

Ethanol vapour travels to the .... where it is

.... **(4 marks)**

Carboxylic acids

1 Distilled vinegar is a colourless solution of ethanoic acid, CH_3COOH. Name an indicator that can be used to show that distilled vinegar is acidic, and give its colour in the vinegar.

> Make sure that the colour matches the indicator you name.

name of indicator: ....

colour in distilled vinegar: .... **(2 marks)**

2 Ethanoic acid has the typical properties of an acid.

(a) Magnesium ribbon reacts with dilute ethanoic acid. Bubbles of gas are produced.

Name the gas produced in the reaction.

> This gas is produced when a metal reacts with water or any dilute acid.

.... **(1 mark)**

(b) Describe what you would see when a small piece of solid sodium carbonate is added to dilute ethanoic acid in a test tube.

....

.... **(2 marks)**

3 The diagram shows the structure of ethanoic acid.

(a) Identify the functional group in carboxylic acids by drawing a circle around it in the diagram.

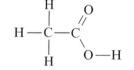

(1 mark)

(b) Methanoic acid molecules each contain one carbon atom. Give the formula of methanoic acid.

> Remember that neighbouring members of an homologous series differ by CH_2.

.... **(1 mark)**

> Guided

(c) Draw the structure of propanoic acid, CH_3CH_2COOH.

(1 mark)

4 Ethanol reacts with an oxidising mixture to form ethanoic acid.

> You do **not** need to know the substances in the oxidising mixture.

Name the carboxylic acid produced when butanol reacts with the oxidising mixture.

> Look at the names of the alcohol and carboxylic acid given in the stem of the question.

.... **(1 mark)**

Investigating combustion

1 A student uses the combustion of different alcohols to heat a container of water. The photo shows the apparatus that she uses.

(a) Combustion is an exothermic reaction. State what is meant by an **exothermic** reaction.

....

.... **(1 mark)**

(b) Give one improvement that the student could make to prevent the thermometer falling over.

....

.... **(1 mark)**

(c) Give a reason why it would be unsafe to move a spirit burner while its wick is alight.

> The alcohols in the spirit burners are highly flammable liquids.

....

.... **(1 mark)**

(d) The student keeps the volume of water the same each time. This is so that she can make a fair comparison between different alcohols. Give one other variable that the student should control.

> This should be a variable or factor that also affects the measured temperature increase in the water.

.... **(1 mark)**

2 The table shows the results of an investigation involving two alcohols.

Fuel	Starting temperature of the water (°C)	Final temperature of the water (°C)	Change in temperature of the water (°C)	Mass of fuel burned (g)
ethanol	18	42		0.40
butanol	18	47		0.43

(a) Complete the table to show the changes in the temperature of the water. **(1 mark)**

Guided

(b) Determine which fuel produces the greatest change in temperature per gram of fuel burned.

ethanol: (42 – 18)/0.40 = ...

butanol: ....

So .... produces the greatest change per gram of fuel. **(2 marks)**

Nanoparticles

1 Which of the following is approximately the same size as a nanoparticle?

Object	Approximate size (nm)
☐ A carbon atom	0.3
☐ B cold virus	30
☐ C bacterium	1000
☐ D red blood cell	8000

(1 mark)

2 Fool's gold is iron sulfide, FeS_2. It forms gold-coloured cubic crystals.

A fool's gold crystal is found to have sides 10 mm long.

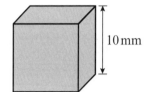

10 mm

> **Guided**

(a) Calculate the total surface area of this cube.

$10 \times 10 \times 6 =$ .... mm^2 **(1 mark)**

> **Guided**

(b) Calculate the volume of this cube.

$10 \times 10 \times 10 =$ .... mm^3 **(1 mark)**

(c) Calculate the surface area:volume ratio of this cube.

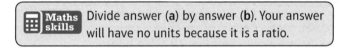
Maths skills Divide answer **(a)** by answer **(b)**. Your answer will have no units because it is a ratio.

.... **(1 mark)**

3 Titanium dioxide is a white solid when in bulk. It absorbs harmful ultraviolet radiation present in sunlight. Nanoparticulate titanium dioxide also absorbs ultraviolet light but is transparent. Experiments show that titanium dioxide nanoparticles do not easily pass into undamaged skin.

(a) Give one reason why someone may prefer a sunscreen containing nanoparticulate titanium dioxide rather than one containing bulk titanium dioxide.

.... **(1 mark)**

(b) Some scientists are worried about the possible effects of titanium dioxide nanoparticles on human health.

(i) Give one way in which nanoparticles could enter the human body.

.... **(1 mark)**

(ii) Suggest one reason to explain why nanoparticles might cause harmful reactions in body cells.

Think about the typical chemical properties of nanoparticles.

.... **(1 mark)**

> **Guided**

(c) Titanium dioxide nanoparticles are the catalyst for a self-cleaning coating for window glass. Explain why nanoparticles may be more effective catalysts than the same substances in bulk.

Nanoparticles have a very large ....

so reactant particles .... **(2 marks)**

Bulk materials

1   Which of the following rows in the table correctly shows a typical property of each material?

> It may help if you look at the properties of each material in turn, rather than looking across each row.

	Glass	Clay ceramics	Polymers	Metals
☐ A	hard	brittle	good conductor of electricity	good conductor of electricity
☐ B	transparent	opaque	poor conductor of heat	brittle
☐ C	poor conductor of heat	poor conductor of electricity	poor conductor of electricity	dull when polished
☐ D	poor conductor of electricity	poor conductor of heat	poor conductor of heat	ductile

(1 mark)

2   The table shows some properties of four metals.

Metal	Melting point (°C)	Density (kg/m³)	Relative electrical conductivity	Relative hardness
chromium	1857	7200	0.8	8.5
copper	1083	8900	6.4	3.0
iron	1535	7900	1.1	4.0
zinc	420	7100	1.8	2.5

(a) Identify the metal in the table which:

(i) has the highest density

(ii) is the softest.

.... **(1 mark)**   .... **(1 mark)**

(b) Give one reason, using information from the table, why copper is used to make electrical cables.

> Choose the most relevant property from the table.

.... **(1 mark)**

(c) Some drill bits can drill through sheets of metal. Friction causes heating during drilling. Give **two** reasons, using information from the table, why chromium may be suitable for making a drill bit.

1: ....

2: .... **(2 marks)**

3   Car windscreens are made from a composite material. This consists of a thin sheet of tough, transparent polymer glued between two thicker sheets of glass.

(a) State one physical property that a car windscreen should have, and give a reason for your answer.

property: ....

reason: .... **(2 marks)**

(b) Describe an advantage of using the composite material compared with using glass alone.

> Think about a disadvantage of glass alone, especially in the event of an accident.

....

.... **(2 marks)**

Extended response – Materials

*Car body panels are usually made from steel sheet, pressed into shape. Today, some cars may have body panels made from composite materials. The table shows information about three of these materials.

Material	Cost (£/kg)	Relative strength	Relative stiffness	Brittleness	Notes
FRR	2	0.7	0.6	low	can be coloured can be pressed into shape
fibreglass	4	0.8	0.4	medium	can be coloured must be built up in layers
CRP	42	10	10	high	black must be built up in layers

> The greater the relative strength or stiffness, the stronger or stiffer the material is. A very stiff material is not very flexible.

All three consist of polymer resins reinforced with fibres. FRR contains cotton fibres, fibreglass contains glass fibres and CRP contains carbon fibres.

Evaluate the different composite materials for use in car body panels, such as front wings or doors.

> You need to review the information in the table, and then bring it together to form a conclusion. This will include comparing the strengths and weaknesses of using each material for car body panels.

....

....

....

....

....

....

....

....

....

....

.... **(6 marks)**

> You should be able to explain why the properties of a material make it suitable for a given use, and to use data to select materials appropriate for specific uses.

Timed Test 1

Time allowed: 1 hour 45 minutes

Total marks: 100

Edexcel publishes official Sample Assessment Material on its website. This practice exam paper has been written to help you practise what you have learned and may not be representative of a real exam paper.

Six-mark questions are indicated with a star (*).

1 (a) The table shown in Figure 1 gives the numbers of protons, neutrons and electrons in five different particles (**V**, **W**, **X**, **Y** and **Z**).

Particle	Protons	Neutrons	Electrons
V	8	8	8
W	11	12	11
X	13	14	10
Y	15	16	18
Z	18	22	18

Figure 1

(i) Which particle is a positively charged **ion**?

☐ **A** particle W

☐ **B** particle X

☐ **C** particle Y

☐ **D** particle Z **(1 mark)**

(ii) Which particles are **atoms** of non-metals?

☐ **A** particles V and W

☐ **B** particles W and X

☐ **C** particles X and Y

☐ **D** particles V and Z **(1 mark)**

(b) Complete the table shown in Figure 2 to show the properties of protons, neutrons and electrons.

Subatomic particle	Relative mass	Relative charge
proton	1	
neutron		
electron		−1

Figure 2 **(4 marks)**

(c) Neon has the atomic number 10. Neon exists as neon-20 and neon-22 atoms.

Explain, in terms of protons and neutrons, why these atoms are isotopes of neon. **(2 marks)**

(Total for Question 1 = 8 marks)

2 This question is about elements and the periodic table.

(a) Which of these describes the arrangement of elements in the modern periodic table?

☐ **A** in order of increasing relative atomic mass

☐ **B** in order of increasing relative formula mass

☐ **C** in order of increasing mass number

☐ **D** in order of increasing atomic number **(1 mark)**

(b) Dmitri Mendeleev (1834–1907) was a Russian chemist who developed a periodic table.

Give one similarity and one difference between Mendeleev's table and the modern periodic table. **(2 marks)**

(c) Phosphorus, P, has the atomic number 15. Complete the diagram below to show the electronic configuration of phosphorus.

(1 mark)

(d) The table shown in Figure 3 gives the numbers of electrons in atoms of lithium, sodium and magnesium.

Element	Number of electrons in atom
lithium	3
sodium	11
magnesium	12

Figure 3

Explain, in terms of their electronic configurations, why:

(i) lithium and sodium are placed in group 1 **(1 mark)**

(ii) sodium and magnesium are placed in period 3. **(1 mark)**

(Total for Question 2 = 6 marks)

3 The table shown in Figure 4 gives the formulae of two ions.

Name of ion	Formula of ion
aluminium	Al^{3+}
sulfate	SO_4^{2-}

Figure 4

(a) Which of these is the correct formula for aluminium sulfate?

☐ **A** Al_3SO_4

☐ **B** $Al_3(SO_4)_2$

☐ **C** $Al_2(SO_4)_3$

☐ **D** Al_2SO_4 **(1 mark)**

(b) The atomic number of aluminium is 13 and its mass number is 27.

Calculate the numbers of protons, neutrons and electrons in an aluminium **ion**. **(3 marks)**

(c)   The melting point of aluminium sulfate is 770°C.

Explain why the melting point of aluminium sulfate is high. **(3 marks)**

(d)   Aluminium sulfate is soluble in water. It is used in the treatment of water for drinking.

A solution of aluminium sulfate is formed by dissolving 35 g of aluminium sulfate in 250 cm³ of water. Calculate the concentration, in g dm⁻³, of this solution. **(2 marks)**

(Total for Question 3 = 9 marks)

4 Air is a mixture of gases, including nitrogen, oxygen and carbon dioxide.

(a)   Why does nitrogen have a low boiling point?

☐ **A** There are weak forces of attraction between nitrogen molecules.

☐ **B** There are weak covalent bonds between nitrogen molecules.

☐ **C** There are weak forces of attraction between nitrogen atoms.

☐ **D** There are weak covalent bonds between nitrogen atoms. **(1 mark)**

(b)   The structure of a water molecule can be shown as:

H–O–H

The symbol – is used to show a covalent bond.

The electronic configuration of hydrogen is 1 and the electronic configuration of oxygen is 2.6.

Draw a dot-and-cross diagram to show a molecule of water, H_2O.

Show the outer electrons only. **(2 marks)**

(c)   Figure 5 shows the structures of diamond and graphite.

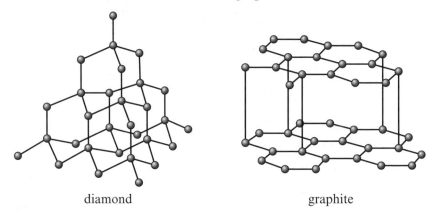

diamond   graphite

Figure 5

Explain, in terms of structure and bonding, why:

(i) diamond has a very high melting point **(2 marks)**

(ii) graphite is used as a lubricant. **(3 marks)**

(Total for Question 4 = 8 marks)

5 A student adds magnesium to an excess of dilute hydrochloric acid in an evaporating basin. Magnesium chloride solution and hydrogen gas form. When the reaction is complete, the student carefully evaporates the magnesium chloride solution to dryness. The table in Figure 6 shows her results.

Substance	Mass (g)
magnesium used	2.40
magnesium chloride formed	9.50

Figure 6

(a)   Describe two things happening in the reaction that the student would see. **(2 marks)**

(b)   Describe the chemical test for hydrogen. **(2 marks)**

(c) Use the information in the table to calculate the mass of chlorine present in the magnesium chloride. **(1 mark)**

(d) Use the mass of magnesium used (shown in the table) and your answer to part (c) to calculate the empirical formula of magnesium chloride.

(A_r of Mg = 24.0 and A_r of Cl = 35.5) **(3 marks)**

(Total for Question 5 = 8 marks)

6 This question is about clean tap water.

(a) Which of these describes clean tap water?

☐ **A** a pure substance

☐ **B** a simple molecular compound

☐ **C** a mixture of substances

☐ **D** not potable **(1 mark)**

(b) Complete the table shown in Figure 7 to describe the arrangement and movement of particles in each of the three states of matter.

State	Arrangement of particles	Movement of particles
solid		
liquid	close together random	
gas		rapid in all directions

Figure 7 **(4 marks)**

(c) Drinking water can be made by the simple distillation of seawater.

(i) State, in terms of the relative energy of water particles, what happens when water is heated. **(1 mark)**

(ii) Suggest a reason to explain why producing large volumes of drinking water by simple distillation is expensive. **(1 mark)**

(iii) Tap water contains dissolved salts that may interfere with chemical tests. Describe why distilled water is suitable for use in such tests. **(1 mark)**

(d) Fresh water can be made safe for drinking at a water treatment plant. Sedimentation is needed to allow very small particles to settle out. Filtration and chlorination are also needed.

(i) Describe why filtration is needed. **(1 mark)**

(ii) Explain why chlorination is needed. **(2 marks)**

(Total for Question 6 = 11 marks)

7 This question is about acids, alkalis and salts.

(a) Which row in the table is correct?

	Soluble in water	Insoluble in water
☐ **A**	silver chloride	lead chloride
☐ **B**	sodium carbonate	calcium sulfate
☐ **C**	sodium chloride	calcium chloride
☐ **D**	barium sulfate	barium nitrate

(1 mark)

(b) Predict whether a precipitate will form when sodium hydroxide solution and iron(III) chloride solution are mixed together. Name any precipitate that forms. **(1 mark)**

(c) Copper oxide and potassium hydroxide are examples of bases.

    (i) Give a reason why both substances are bases. **(1 mark)**

    (ii) Give a reason why potassium hydroxide is also described as an alkali. **(1 mark)**

(d) Aqueous solutions can be acidic, neutral or alkaline.

    (i) Give the pH of a neutral solution. **(1 mark)**

    (ii) Give the name of the type of aqueous solution that contains an excess of hydrogen ions, $H^+(aq)$. **(1 mark)**

*(e) Plan an experiment to prepare pure, dry crystals of copper chloride, $CuCl_2$, from an insoluble copper compound and a suitable dilute acid. In your answer, include the names of suitable reagents and describe any essential stages. You may wish to write an equation to help with your plan. **(6 marks)**

(Total for Question 7 = 12 marks)

8 This question is about electrolysis and electroplating.

(a) State what is meant by the term '**electrolyte**'. **(2 marks)**

(b) Which of the following correctly describes the movement of ions during electrolysis?

    ☐ **A** Negatively charged cations migrate to the positively charged cathode.

    ☐ **B** Positively charged cations migrate to the negatively charged cathode.

    ☐ **C** Positively charged anions migrate to the negatively charged anode.

    ☐ **D** Positively charged anions migrate to the positively charged anode. **(1 mark)**

(c) Two products form during the electrolysis of a concentrated sodium sulfate solution.

Which row in the table correctly shows what product forms at each electrode?

		Cathode	Anode
☐	**A**	sodium	oxygen
☐	**B**	sodium	hydrogen
☐	**C**	hydrogen	oxygen
☐	**D**	hydrogen	sodium

(1 mark)

(d) Predict the product formed at each electrode during the electrolysis of molten zinc chloride. **(2 marks)**

(e) Aluminium is extracted by the electrolysis of aluminium oxide, dissolved in molten cryolite.

State why aluminium cannot be extracted from aluminium oxide by heating with carbon. **(1 mark)**

(f) Metal objects can be electroplated with a thin layer of another metal.

    (i) State **two** reasons why this may be done. **(2 marks)**

    (ii) Steel cutlery can be electroplated with silver. Describe the necessary anode, cathode and electrolyte needed to do this. **(2 marks)**

(Total for Question 8 = 11 marks)

9 This question is about metals.

(a) Iron is a transition metal. Which of the following is a **typical** property of transition metals?

☐ **A** They form colourless compounds.

☐ **B** They have low densities.

☐ **C** They rust in air and water.

☐ **D** They have high melting points. **(1 mark)**

(b) Copper can be extracted by heating copper oxide, CuO, with carbon. Copper and carbon dioxide form.

(i) Balance the equation for the reaction.

......CuO + C → ......Cu + CO_2 **(1 mark)**

(ii) A student heats some copper oxide with carbon. The theoretical yield is 2.95 g of copper but his actual yield is 2.36 g. Calculate the percentage yield of copper. **(2 marks)**

(iii) Give **two** reasons why the actual yield of a reaction is usually less than the theoretical yield. **(2 marks)**

(c) Copper can also be extracted by heating copper(I) sulfide in air:
Cu_2S + O_2 → $2Cu$ + SO_2

Calculate the atom economy of producing copper using this reaction.

(A_r of Cu = 63.5, A_r of S = 32.0 and A_r of O = 16.0) **(3 marks)**

(Total for Question 9 = 9 marks)

10 Ammonia is manufactured from nitrogen and hydrogen by the Haber process:

$$N_2(g) + 3H_2(g) \rightleftharpoons 2NH_3(g)$$

(a) Give the meaning of the symbol $\rightleftharpoons$ in chemical equations. **(1 mark)**

(b) State the conditions used in the Haber process:

(i) temperature **(1 mark)**

(ii) pressure **(1 mark)**

(iii) catalyst **(1 mark)**

(c) Ammonia is used to make salts for fertilisers. Ammonium nitrate, NH_4NO_3, is one of these salts. It is a source of soluble nitrogen needed to promote plant growth.

(i) Name one element, other than nitrogen, that fertilisers may contain to promote plant growth. **(1 mark)**

(ii) Name the acid that reacts with ammonia to form ammonium nitrate. **(1 mark)**

(d) Ammonium sulfate, $(NH_4)_2SO_4$, is a soluble salt used as a fertiliser. It is made by reacting ammonia solution with dilute sulfuric acid.

(i) Name the other product formed in the reaction. **(1 mark)**

(ii) Explain why titration must be used to prepare ammonium sulfate solution. **(2 marks)**

(Total for Question 10 = 9 marks)

11 This question is about chemical cells and fuel cells.

(a) The voltage of a Daniell cell, a type of chemical cell, is 1.1 V. Give a reason why this voltage decreases when the cell is left connected in an electrical circuit. **(1 mark)**

(b) Hydrogen–oxygen fuel cells produce a voltage for as long as they are supplied with hydrogen, H_2, and oxygen, O_2. Write the balanced equation for the overall reaction that happens in these fuel cells. **(2 marks)**

*(c) Warehouses are used to store goods and materials so that they can be distributed to shops and factories. Forklift trucks move heavy containers from place to place in warehouses. Many warehouses are large buildings but may have narrow spaces. Forklift trucks may be powered by rechargeable batteries, diesel engines or hydrogen–oxygen fuel cells.

Figure 8 shows some features of these three ways to power forklift trucks.

Feature	Rechargeable batteries	Diesel engines	Hydrogen–oxygen fuel cells
noise in use	quiet	noisy	quiet
emissions in use	none	carbon monoxide, smoke, water vapour	water vapour
approximate time to recharge or refuel	12 hours	3 minutes	5 minutes
size	smallest	largest	medium-sized

Figure 8

Use the information from the table to evaluate the strengths and weaknesses of hydrogen–oxygen fuel cells for use in forklift trucks.

(6 marks)

(Total for Question 11 = 9 marks)

TOTAL FOR PAPER = 100 marks

Timed Test 2

Time allowed: 1 hour 45 minutes

Total marks: 100

Edexcel publishes official Sample Assessment Material on its website. This practice exam paper has been written to help you practise what you have learned and may not be representative of a real exam paper.

Six-mark questions are indicated with a star (*).

1 This question is about the alkali metals, the elements in group 1 of the periodic table.

(a) Which of these shows the typical physical properties of the alkali metals?

☐ **A** soft with relatively low melting points

☐ **B** soft with relatively high melting points

☐ **C** hard with relatively low melting points

☐ **D** hard with relatively high melting points   **(1 mark)**

(b) Sodium reacts with water to produce sodium hydroxide solution, NaOH, and hydrogen gas, H_2.

(i) Balance the equation for the reaction between sodium and water. Include state symbols.   **(2 marks)**

(ii) Describe **two** observations seen when a piece of sodium is added to a trough of water.   **(2 marks)**

(c) The table in Figure 1 shows the atomic numbers and electronic configurations of lithium and sodium.

Element	Atomic number	Electronic configuration
lithium	3	2.1
sodium	11	2.8.1

Figure 1

(i) The atomic number of potassium is 19. Write the electronic configuration of potassium.   **(1 mark)**

(ii) Explain, in terms of their electronic configurations, why sodium is more reactive than lithium.   **(3 marks)**

(Total for Question 1 = 9 marks)

2 This question is about the halogens, the elements in group 7 of the periodic table.

(a) Which row in the table correctly shows the colours and physical states of the halogens at room temperature and pressure?

	Chlorine	Bromine	Iodine
☐ **A**	pale-yellow liquid	red–brown liquid	red–brown solid
☐ **B**	yellow–green gas	dark-grey liquid	dark-grey solid
☐ **C**	yellow–green gas	red–brown liquid	dark-grey solid
☐ **D**	yellow–green gas	purple liquid	red–brown liquid

                                                                    (1 mark)

(b) Describe a chemical test for chlorine.   **(2 marks)**

*(c)   A student investigates the reactivity of the halogens. She adds a few drops of a dilute aqueous solution of bromine to potassium iodide solution, and then to potassium chloride solution. Her results are shown in the table below (Figure 2).

Mixture	Observation
bromine + potassium iodide	colour change seen
bromine + potassium chloride	no visible change

Figure 2

Explain how the student's observations provide evidence for the order of reactivity of bromine, iodine and chlorine. You should include an equation in your answer.   **(6 marks)**

(Total for Question 2 = 9 marks)

3 A student investigates the rate of reaction between calcium carbonate (marble chips) and excess dilute hydrochloric acid: $CaCO_3(s) + 2HCl(aq) \rightarrow CaCl_2(aq) + H_2O(l) + CO_2(g)$

(a)   Which of these would increase the rate of the reaction?

☐ **A** adding water to the acid

☐ **B** increasing the volume of acid

☐ **C** increasing the size of the marble chips

☐ **D** using calcium carbonate powder instead of marble chips   **(1 mark)**

(b)   Describe the chemical test for carbon dioxide.   **(2 marks)**

(c)   The temperature of the reaction mixture increases during the reaction. Explain what this tells you about the reaction between calcium carbonate and dilute hydrochloric acid.   **(2 marks)**

(d)   The student measured the volume of carbon dioxide produced until all the calcium carbonate had reacted. Figure 3 shows the results that he obtained at 20 °C.

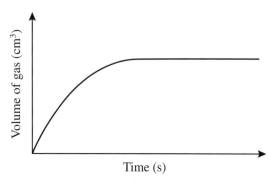

Figure 3

(i)   Sketch, on the same axes above, the results that the student would obtain by repeating the experiment with a higher concentration of hydrochloric acid at 20 °C.   **(2 marks)**

(ii)   Explain, in terms of particles, why increasing the concentration of hydrochloric acid has this effect on the rate of reaction.   **(2 marks)**

(iii) State the effect on the reaction time of increasing the temperature of the reaction mixture.   **(1 mark)**

(Total for Question 3 = 10 marks)

4 Reactions involve energy transfers to and from the surroundings.

(a)   Which row in the table correctly shows the types of energy changes involved in breaking chemical bonds and forming chemical bonds?

		Breaking bonds	Forming bonds
□	A	exothermic	endothermic
□	B	exothermic	exothermic
□	C	endothermic	endothermic
□	D	endothermic	exothermic

(1 mark)

(b) Explain what is meant by the term '**activation energy**'. **(2 marks)**

(c) Hydrogen peroxide decomposes to form water and oxygen:

$2H_2O_2(aq) \rightarrow 2H_2O(l) + O_2(g)$

The reaction is exothermic.

Draw and label the reaction profile diagram for this reaction, clearly labelling the activation energy.

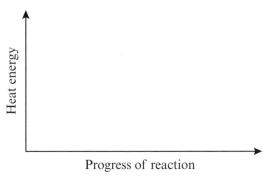

(3 marks)

(d) (i) On the same axes above, draw the reaction profile for the same reaction in the presence of a catalyst. Label this reaction profile with an **X**. **(1 mark)**

(ii) The products formed in a reaction are the same whether or not a catalyst is used.

State **two** other features of a catalyst. **(2 marks)**

(e) Describe the role of enzymes in the production of alcoholic drinks. **(1 mark)**

(Total for Question 4 = 10 marks)

5 This question is about crude oil.

(a) Which of these statements about crude oil is correct?

□ A It is a renewable resource.

□ B It contains molecules with carbon atoms in rings and chains.

□ C It is a complex mixture of carbohydrates.

□ D At room temperature, it contains only liquids. **(1 mark)**

(b) Crude oil is separated in fractions using fractional distillation. Figure 4 shows an oil fractionation column and the main fractions obtained from it.

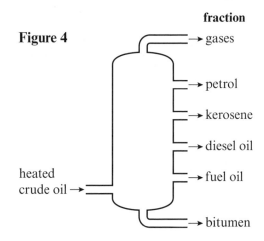

Figure 4

(i) Identify the fraction that has the highest boiling point. **(1 mark)**

(ii) Identify the fraction that is used as a fuel for large ships and some power stations. **(1 mark)**

(iii) Give a commercial use for the kerosene fraction. **(1 mark)**

(c) Give one industrial use of crude oil, other than as a source of fuels. **(1 mark)**

(d) State why crude oil may be described as a finite resource. **(1 mark)**

(e) The substances in crude oil fractions are mostly members of the alkane homologous series.

(i) Describe why alkanes are **hydrocarbons**. **(2 marks)**

(ii) The hydrocarbons in different fractions have different boiling points. State **two** other ways in which they differ. **(2 marks)**

(Total for Question 5 = 10 marks)

6 This question is about the Earth's atmosphere.

(a) Where do scientists think the gases in the Earth's earliest atmosphere came from?

☐ **A** the oceans

☐ **B** primitive plants

☐ **C** carbonate rocks

☐ **D** volcanoes **(1 mark)**

(b) Which gas was the most abundant in the Earth's earliest atmosphere?

☐ **A** nitrogen

☐ **B** oxygen

☐ **C** argon

☐ **D** carbon dioxide **(1 mark)**

(c) Oxygen is found in the atmosphere.

(i) Describe the chemical test for oxygen. **(2 marks)**

(ii) Explain why the amount of oxygen in the atmosphere increased over millions of years. **(2 marks)**

(d) Carbon dioxide is described as a greenhouse gas.

(i) Explain how the formation of oceans affected the amount of carbon dioxide in the atmosphere. **(2 marks)**

(ii) Human activities increase the amount of some greenhouse gases. Complete the table below.

Name of greenhouse gas	Main human activity that produces the gas
carbon dioxide	
	livestock farming

(2 marks)

(iii) Increasing amounts of greenhouse gases in the atmosphere cause global warming. Other than an increase in temperature, describe one potential effect of global warming on the environment. **(1 mark)**

(Total for Question 6 = 11 marks)

7 This question is about the combustion of hydrocarbon fuels.

(a) Which row in the table correctly shows the possible products of complete combustion and incomplete combustion of hydrocarbon fuels?

	Complete combustion	Incomplete combustion
☐ A	carbon dioxide, water	carbon monoxide only
☐ B	carbon dioxide, carbon monoxide, water	carbon monoxide, water
☐ C	carbon dioxide, water	carbon monoxide, carbon, water
☐ D	carbon monoxide, water	carbon dioxide, carbon, water

(1 mark)

(b) Sulfur dioxide is produced when some hydrocarbon fuels burn.

(i) Name the element that reacts with oxygen to produce sulfur dioxide. **(1 mark)**

(ii) Acid rain forms when sulfur dioxide dissolves in water in the atmosphere.

Describe **two** environmental problems caused by acid rain. **(2 marks)**

(c) Oxides of nitrogen are pollutants. Nitrogen dioxide, NO_2, is one of these pollutant gases. It is produced when fuels are burned in engines.

(i) Write a balanced equation for the reaction between nitrogen gas and oxygen gas to produce nitrogen dioxide. Include state symbols in your answer. **(3 marks)**

(ii) State where the nitrogen and oxygen, needed to produce oxides of nitrogen, come from. **(1 mark)**

(iii) Describe the reaction condition in engines that allows nitrogen and oxygen to react together. **(1 mark)**

(d) Carbon monoxide may be produced during the combustion of hydrocarbon fuels. Explain how it acts as a toxic gas. **(2 marks)**

(Total for Question 7 = 11 marks)

8 This question is about tests for ions.

(a) Which ion gives a blue–green flame test result?

☐ A calcium, Ca^{2+}

☐ B copper, Cu^{2+}

☐ C potassium, K^+

☐ D ammonium, NH_4^+ **(1 mark)**

(b) Halide ions can be identified using dilute nitric acid and silver nitrate solution. Which row in the table gives the correct colours of the silver halide precipitates formed in these chemical tests?

	Silver chloride	Silver bromide	Silver iodide
☐ A	white	yellow	cream
☐ B	yellow	cream	white
☐ C	white	cream	yellow
☐ D	white	pale green	yellow

(1 mark)

(c) Two metal compounds (**A** and **B**) are tested separately using flame tests, dilute hydrochloric acid, and acidified barium chloride solution. The table (Figure 5) shows the results of all these tests.

Metal compound	Flame test	Dilute hydrochloric acid	Barium chloride solution
A	yellow	brief bubbling seen	no visible change
B	red	no visible change	white precipitate forms

Figure 5

Deduce the names of compounds **A** and **B**. (4 marks)

*(d) You are given three soluble powders: iron(II) chloride, aluminium chloride and calcium chloride.

Describe how you could use dilute sodium hydroxide solution to identify the metal ions present in each of the powders. In your answer, include what you would do and what you would expect to see. (6 marks)

(**Total for Question 8 = 12 marks**)

9 The molecules contained in a substance can be modelled in different ways. Figure 6 shows some information taken from a chemistry textbook.

Chemical formulae for ethene

Molecular formula	Empirical formula	Structural formula	Structure
C_2H_4	CH_2	$CH_2{=}CH_2$	$\begin{array}{c} H \quad\quad H \\ \diagdown \quad\quad \diagup \\ C{=}C \\ \diagup \quad\quad \diagdown \\ H \quad\quad H \end{array}$

Figure 6

(a) The molecular formula of butane is C_4H_{10}. What is its empirical formula?

☐ **A** C_4H_{10}

☐ **B** C_2H_5

☐ **C** $CH_{2.5}$

☐ **D** $C_{0.4}H$ (1 mark)

(b) The structural formula of but-2-ene is $CH_3CH{=}CHCH_3$.

(i) Deduce the molecular formula of but-2-ene. (1 mark)

(ii) Draw the structure of but-2-ene, showing all the covalent bonds. (2 marks)

(c) Ethane, C_2H_6, is a saturated hydrocarbon. Ethene, C_2H_4, is an unsaturated hydrocarbon.

(i) Describe why ethene is unsaturated. (1 mark)

(ii) Explain how bromine water may be used to distinguish between ethane and ethene. (2 marks)

(d)   Ethene reacts with bromine. Which row in the table correctly describes the reaction?

	Type of reaction	Product formed
☐ A	addition	CH_2BrCH_2Br
☐ B	addition	CH_3CH_2Br
☐ C	oxidation	CH_2BrCH_2Br
☐ D	oxidation	CH_3CH_2Br

(1 mark)

(Total for Question 9 = 8 marks)

10 This question is about polymers.

(a)   DNA, starch and proteins are naturally occurring polymers. Which row in the table correctly shows their monomers?

	DNA	Starch	Proteins
☐ A	fatty acids	sugars	amino acids
☐ B	nucleotides	amino acids	fatty acids
☐ C	sugars	amino acids	nucleotides
☐ D	nucleotides	sugars	amino acids

(1 mark)

(b)   Explain what is meant by the term '**polymer**'.   **(2 marks)**

(c)   Figure 7 shows the structure of propene.

Figure 7

(i)   Name the polymer formed by propene.   **(1 mark)**

(ii) Draw the structure of the repeating unit of the polymer formed by propene.   **(2 marks)**

(iii) Name the products of the complete combustion of propene.   **(2 marks)**

(d)   Explain one problem caused by the disposal of polymers.   **(2 marks)**

(Total for Question 10 = 10 marks)

TOTAL FOR PAPER = 100 marks

Answers

1. Formulae

1 C **(1)**

2 first box ticked **(1)**, last box ticked **(1)**

3 1 mark for each correct formula: water, H_2O; carbon dioxide, CO_2; methane, CH_4; sulfuric acid, H_2SO_4; sodium, Na

4 An element is a substance made from atoms **(1)** with the same number of protons **(1)**.

5 (a) 3 **(1)**

　 (b) 7 **(1)**

6 (a) There is a negative sign in the formula. **(1)**

　 (b) The 3 shows that there are three oxygen atoms **(1)**; the 2 shows that the ion has two (negative) charges **(1)**.

2. Equations

1 B **(1)**

2 table completed to show: copper carbonate – reactant **(1)**; copper oxide *and* carbon dioxide – product **(1)**

3 sodium hydroxide + hydrochloric acid $\rightarrow$ sodium chloride + water **(1)**

4 1 mark for all four state symbols in the correct order: (s), (l), (aq), (g)

5 1 mark for each correctly balanced equation:

　 (a) $2Cu + O_2 \rightarrow 2CuO$ **(1)**

　 (b) $2Al + Fe_2O_3 \rightarrow Al_2O_3 + 2Fe$ **(1)**

　 (c) $Mg + 2HNO_3 \rightarrow Mg(NO_3)_2 + H_2$ **(1)**

　 (d) $Na_2CO_3 + 2HCl \rightarrow 2NaCl + H_2O + CO_2$ **(1)**

　 (e) $Cl_2 + 2NaBr \rightarrow 2NaCl + Br_2$ **(1)**

　 (f) $4Fe + 3O_2 \rightarrow 2Fe_2O_3$ **(1)**

3. Hazards, risk and precautions

1 1 mark for each correct new line (if more than four new lines drawn, subtract 1 mark for each extra line):

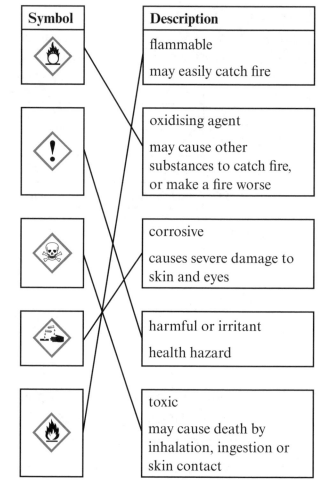

Symbol	Description
	flammable may easily catch fire
	oxidising agent may cause other substances to catch fire, or make a fire worse
	corrosive causes severe damage to skin and eyes
	harmful or irritant health hazard
	toxic may cause death by inhalation, ingestion or skin contact

2 to indicate the dangers associated with the contents **(1)**; to inform people about safe-working precautions with these substances **(1)**

3 A hazard is something that could cause damage/harm to someone/something **(1)** or cause adverse health effects **(1)**.

4 Risk is the chance that someone or something will be harmed **(1)** if exposed to a hazard **(1)**.

5 (a) suitable precaution, e.g. wear gloves/work in a fume cupboard **(1)**

　 (b) reason to match the precaution in part (**a**), e.g. to avoid skin contact because nitric acid is corrosive/to avoid breathing in nitrogen dioxide (which is toxic) **(1)**

4. Atomic structure

1 D **(1)**

2 A **(1)**

3 1 mark for each correct row:

	Protons	Neutrons	Electrons
Nucleus	✓	✓	
Shells			✓

4 2 or 3 correct **(1)**, 4 correct (2)

Particle	proton	neutron	electron
Relative mass	1	1	1/1836
Relative charge	+1	0	−1

5 Protons and electrons have equal but opposite charges/the relative charge of a proton is +1 and the relative charge of an electron is −1 **(1)**; these charges cancel out/add up to zero **(1)**.

6 These particles were not discovered until later. **(1)**

5. Isotopes

1 The mass number of an atom is the total number of protons and neutrons (in the nucleus). **(1)**

2 A **(1)**

3 An element consists of atoms that have the same number of protons **(1)** in the nucleus, and this is different for different elements **(1)**.

4 (a) 1 mark for each correct row:

Isotope	Protons	Neutrons	Electrons
hydrogen-1	1	0	1
hydrogen-2	1	1	1
hydrogen-3	1	2	1

 (b) Isotopes of an element have atoms with the same number of protons **(1)** but different numbers of neutrons **(1)**.

5 Some elements have different isotopes **(1)** so their relative atomic masses are a (weighted) mean value **(1)**.

6. Mendeleev's table

1 (a) D **(1)**

 (b) the properties of the elements and their compounds **(1)**

2 (a) one of the following for 1 mark: Elements are in groups; elements are in periods; elements with similar properties are in the same groups.

 (b) (i) two of the following for 1 mark each: Mendeleev's table had fewer elements; did not include the noble gases; was arranged in order of increasing relative atomic mass (not atomic number); did not have a block of transition metals; silver/copper in Group 1; had two elements in some spaces.

 (ii) He could predict the properties of undiscovered elements. **(1)**

3 Tellurium has a greater/higher relative atomic mass than iodine does **(1)**.

 However, iodine atoms have more protons than tellurium atoms do **(1)**.

7. The periodic table

1 B **(1)**

2 (a) group **(1)**

 (b) **A** and **B** **(1)**

 (c) **A, B, C, D** (all four for 1 mark)

 (d) **B** and **E** **(1)**

3 (a) the position of an element on the periodic table **(1)**

 (b) the number of protons **(1)** in an atom's nucleus **(1)**

8. Electronic configurations

1 (a) 2.1 **(1)**

 (b) There are three electrons, so there must be three protons **(1)**, so the four shaded circles must be neutrons **(1)**.

 (c) two shells **(1)**; two electrons in first shell, six in the second **(1)**, e.g.

2 (a) Both have 7 electrons **(1)** in their outer shell **(1)**.

 (b) Fluorine has two occupied shells **(1)** but chlorine has three **(1)**.

3 (a) 2.8.5 **(1)**

 (b) 2.8.8.2 **(1)**

4 group 0 **(1)** because it has a full outer shell **(1)**

Answers

9. Ions

1 D **(1)**

2 (a) 12 – 2 = 10 **(1)**

   (b) 2.8.8 **(1)**

3 1 mark for each correct row:

Ion	Atomic number	Mass number	Protons	Neutrons	Electrons
N^{3-}	7	15	7	8	10
K^+	19	39	**19**	**21**	**18**
Ca^{2+}	20	40	**20**	**20**	**18**
S^{2-}	16	32	**16**	**16**	**18**
Br^-	35	80	**35**	**46**	**36**

4 three shells and 2.8.7 electrons in the chlorine atom **(1)**; three shells and 2.8.8 electrons in the chloride ion **(1)**; brackets with negative sign **(1)**, e.g.

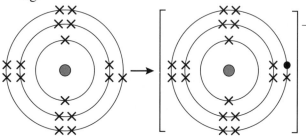

10. Formulae of ionic compounds

1 D **(1)**

2 1 mark for each correct formula:

	Cl^-	S^{2-}	OH^-	NO_3^-	SO_4^{2-}
K^+	KCl	K_2S	KOH	KNO_3	K_2SO_4
Ca^{2+}	$CaCl_2$	CaS	$Ca(OH)_2$	$Ca(NO_3)_2$	$CaSO_4$
Fe^{3+}	$FeCl_3$	Fe_2S_3	$Fe(OH)_3$	$Fe(NO_3)_3$	$Fe_2(SO_4)_3$
NH_4^+	NH_4Cl	$(NH_4)_2S$	NH_4OH	NH_4NO_3	$(NH_4)_2SO_4$

3 (a) $2Mg + O_2 \rightarrow 2MgO$ **(1)**

   (b) (i) The nitrogen atom has five electrons in its outer shell **(1)**; it gains three electrons to complete its outer shell/form an ion **(1)**.

      (ii) Mg_3N_2 **(1)**

      (iii) A nitride ion contains only nitrogen **(1)** but a nitrate ion also contains oxygen **(1)**.

4 1 mark for each correct name:

	S^{2-}	SO_4^{2-}	Cl^-	ClO_3^-
Name	sulfide	sulfate	chloride	chlorate

11. Properties of ionic compounds

1 A **(1)**

2 (a) + and – signs drawn as shown **(1)**

   (b) There are strong electrostatic forces of attraction **(1)** between oppositely charged ions **(1)**.

3 A lot of heat/energy is needed to break/overcome **(1)** the many/strong ionic bonds/bonds between ions **(1)**.

4 (a) liquid *and* dissolved in water are ticked only **(1)**

   (b) must be able to move around **(1)**

12. Covalent bonds

1 C **(1)**

2 A covalent bond forms when a pair of electrons are shared **(1)** between two atoms **(1)**.

3 (a) There is one covalent bond **(1)** between a hydrogen atom and a fluorine atom in a molecule **(1)**.

   (b) correct diagram, e.g.

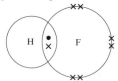

   one pair of dots and crosses in shared area **(1)**; (three) pairs of dots/crosses on F only **(1)**

4 correct diagram, e.g.

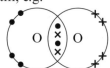

   two pairs of dots and crosses in shared area **(1)**; two pairs of dots on one atom and two pairs of crosses on the other atom **(1)**

13. Simple molecular substances

1 C **(1)**

2 (a) C **(1)**

   (b) two from the following, for 1 mark each: It has a low melting point/lowest melting point; it does not conduct electricity when solid or liquid; it is (almost) insoluble in water.

3 (a) Sulfur hexafluoride molecules are not charged **(1)** and have no electrons that are free to move **(1)**.

(b) The intermolecular forces between water and sulfur hexafluoride molecules **(1)** are weaker than those between water molecules **(1)** and those between sulfur hexafluoride molecules **(1)**.

14. Giant molecular substances

1 B **(1)**

2 (a) carbon **(1)**

(b) four **(1)**

(c) giant molecular/giant covalent **(1)**

3 (a) The layers in graphite can slide over each other **(1)** because there are weak forces between the layers **(1)**.

(b) Atoms in graphite can only form three covalent bonds **(1)** so graphite has electrons that are delocalised/free to move **(1)**.

(c) Diamond has a regular/lattice (1) structure, and its atoms are joined by many strong bonds/covalent bonds **(1)**.

15. Other large molecules

1 C **(1)**

2 (a) carbon **(1)**

(b) covalent **(1)**

3 (a) Its molecules contain 60 atoms/few atoms **(1)** but giant covalent substances contain very many atoms **(1)**.

(b) Buckminsterfullerene has a simple molecular **(1)** structure so it has weak intermolecular forces/forces between molecules **(1)** that are easily overcome.

4 Graphene has covalent **(1)** bonds in a giant/lattice structure **(1)** and these bonds are strong/need a large amount of energy to break **(1)**.

16. Metals

1 A **(1)**

2 1 mark for each correct tick (deduct 1 mark for each tick over four ticks)

	Low melting points	High melting points	Good conductors of electricity	Poor conductors of electricity
Metals		✓	✓	
Non-metals	✓			✓

3 (a) Fizzing is caused by bubbles of hydrogen gas/hydrogen is a gas. **(1)**

(b) Sodium hydroxide dissolves in water **(1)** so the sodium gradually becomes smaller (as the reaction carries on) **(1)**.

4 (a) (i) +/2+ inside the circles **(1)**

(ii) delocalised electrons/sea of electrons shown between the circles **(1)**

(b) It has layers of atoms/(positive) ions **(1)** which can slide over each other **(1)**.

(c) Delocalised electrons/free electrons **(1)** can move through the structure/metal **(1)**.

17. Limitations of models

1 B **(1)**

2 (a) A, B, C **(1)**

(b) A, B **(1)**

(c) C, D **(1)**

(d) B **(1)**

(e) C, D **(1)**

3 (a) Unlike a dot-and-cross diagram, a ball-and-stick model shows the shape of the molecule/can be modelled in three dimensions (e.g. using a modelling kit). **(1)**

(b) Unlike a dot-and-cross diagram, a ball-and-stick model does not show (two of the following, for 1 mark each): the symbols of the elements; the bonding electrons; the non-bonding electrons.

18. Relative formula mass

1 (a) 71 **(1)**

(b) 18 **(1)**

(c) 64 **(1)**

(d) 102 **(1)**

(e) 53.5 **(1)**

(f) 111 **(1)**

(g) 133.5 **(1)**

2 (a) 74 **(1)**

(b) 78 **(1)**

(c) 164 **(1)**

(d) 132 **(1)**

(e) 342 **(1)**

19. Empirical formulae

1 (a) (i) to make sure that the reaction had finished/all the magnesium had reacted **(1)**

(ii) to let air/oxygen in **(1)**

(b) Use tongs/allow the crucible to cool down **(1)** to prevent skin burns **(1)**.

2 mass of oxygen reacted
= 20.65 g − 20.49 g = 0.16 g **(1)**

Mg	O
0.24/24 = 0.010	0.16/16 = 0.010 **(1)**
0.010/0.010 = 1.0	0.010/0.010 = 1.0 **(1)**

Empirical formula is MgO **(1)**

3 M_r of NO_2 = 14 + (2 × 16) = 46 **(1)**

factor needed = 92/46 = 2

Molecular formula is N_2O_4 **(1)**

20. Conservation of mass

1 (a) closed system, because no substances can enter or leave **(1)**

(b) (i) It stays the same. **(1)**

(ii) Mass is conserved in chemical reactions/ atoms are not created or destroyed in chemical reactions. **(1)**

2 8.2 − 5.3 = 2.9 g **(1)**

3 234 g **(1)**

4 M_r of O_2 = 32 and M_r of MgO = 40 **(1)**

(1 × 32) = 32 g of O_2 makes (2 × 40) = 80 g of MgO **(1)**

12.6 g of O_2 makes 80 × (12.6/32) g of MgO = 31.5 g of MgO **(1)**

21. Concentration of solution

1 D **(1)**

2 (a) volume = 2500/1000 = 2.5 dm³ **(1)**

(b) 0.5 dm³ **(1)**

(c) 0.025 dm³ **(1)**

3 (a) 25 g dm⁻³ **(1)**

(b) 36.5 g dm⁻³ **(1)**

(c) 5 g dm⁻³ **(1)**

4 concentration = (10/250) × 1000 = 40 g dm⁻³ **(1)**

5 16 g dm⁻³ **(1)**

6 (a) mixture of a solute and water/solution in which the solvent is water **(1)**

(b) 100 g **(1)**

22. Extended response – Types of substance

The answer may include some of the following points: **(6)**

Graphite uses and properties:

- lubricant because it is slippery/the softest in the table/10 times softer than copper

- electrodes because it is a good conductor of electricity/conductivity is 100 times less than copper/100 million times better than diamond.

diamond uses and properties:

- cutting tools because it is very hard/100 times harder than copper/1000 times harder than graphite.

graphite bonding and structure:

- giant covalent/giant molecular structure

- strong covalent bonds

- Each carbon atom is bonded to three other carbon atoms.

- layers of carbon atoms

- weak forces between layers

- Layers can slide past each other (making it slippery so that it can be used as a lubricant).

- one free electron per carbon atom

- delocalised electrons

- Electrons can move through the structure (allowing it to conduct electricity for use as an electrode).

diamond bonding and structure:

- giant covalent/giant molecular structure

- strong covalent bonds

- Each carbon atom is bonded to four other carbon atoms.

- three-dimensional lattice structure

- A lot of energy is needed to break the many strong bonds.

- rigid structure.

23. States of matter

1 C **(1)**

2 (a) freezing/solidifying **(1)**

(b) condensing/liquefying **(1)**

3 The chemical composition is unchanged. **(1)**

4 1 mark for each correct row in the table, to 3 marks maximum

State of matter	Particles are:			
	Close together	Far apart	Randomly arranged	Regularly arranged
solid	✓			✓
liquid	✓		✓	
gas		✓	✓	

5 (a) gas **(1)**

(b) gas **(1)** because the particles are moving freely/moving fastest/have the most kinetic energy **(1)**

6 liquid **(1)**

7 The arrangement changes from random to regular **(1)** and the movement changes from moving around each other (in groups) to vibrating about fixed positions **(1)**.

24. Pure substances and mixtures

1 D **(1)**

2 The orange juice contains different substances **(1)** mixed together/not chemically joined together **(1)** but a pure substance in the scientific sense contains only one substance/element/compound **(1)**.

3 (a) The atoms of an element all have the same atomic number/number of protons **(1)** but atoms of Na and Cl_2 have different atomic numbers/numbers of protons **(1)**.

(b) substance containing two or more elements **(1)** *chemically* combined/joined together **(1)**

4 (a) **B** 0.24 and **C** 0.03 **(1)**

(b) None of the samples is pure **(1)**; all contain some residue/dissolved solid/solid mixed in **(1)**.

5 Pure substances (e.g. tin and silver) have a sharp melting point **(1)** but mixtures (e.g. lead-free solder) melt over a range of temperatures **(1)**.

25. Distillation

1 C **(1)**

2 (a) (i) condenser **(1)**

(ii) It decreases/goes down. **(1)**

(b) The temperature of the water increases **(1)** because it is heated up by the vapour/energy is transferred from the vapour to the water by heating **(1)**.

3 (a) ethanol because it has a lower boiling point than water **(1)**; it boils/evaporates first **(1)**

(b) one of the following for 1 mark:

- More energy is transferred by heating.

- Hot vapour and cold water flow in opposite directions.

- The condenser will be full of cold water/will not contain any air.

26. Filtration and crystallisation

1 second box ticked **(1)**; fourth box ticked **(1)**
Deduct 1 mark for each extra tick above two ticks.

2 (a) $2KI(aq) + Pb(NO_3)_2(aq) \rightarrow 2KNO_3(aq) + PbI_2(s)$

1 mark for correct balancing; 1 mark for correct state symbols

(b) (i) Its particles are too large to pass through. **(1)**

(ii) to remove excess potassium iodide solution/lead nitrate solution/potassium nitrate solution **(1)**

3 (a) filtration/filtering **(1)**

(b) (i) The *water* evaporates **(1)**; solution becomes saturated/crystals form as more *water* evaporates **(1)**.

(ii) to dry the crystals **(1)**

(c) Heat the solution slowly/do not evaporate all of the water/leave to cool/stop heating before crystals start to form. **(1)**

27. Paper chromatography

1 (a) Pencil does not dissolve in the solvent. **(1)**

(b) mixture because it contains more than one substance/four substances **(1)**; pure substances contain only one substance **(1)**

(c) **A** and **B** **(1)**

(d) The orange squash does contain X because it contains spots with the same R_f values/that move the same distances **(1)** as the two spots in X **(1)**.

(e) It is insoluble in the solvent/it is insoluble in the mobile phase/has very strong bonds with the stationary phase/has very weak bonds with the mobile phase. **(1)**

28. Investigating inks

1 (a) distance travelled by the spot/dye **(1)**; distance travelled by the solvent/solvent front **(1)**

(b) The measurements will be more precise/have a higher resolution **(1)** so the R_f value will be more accurate/closer to the true value **(1)**.

2 (a) to stop the solution boiling over (into the condenser) **(1)** so that the solvent collected is not contaminated with the solution/so that the vapour is not produced faster than it can be condensed **(1)**

(b) The apparatus will get very hot/solvent vapour (e.g. steam) will escape. **(1)**

3 (a) (highly) flammable **(1)**

(b) The student should work in a fume cupboard because the vapour causes dizziness **(1)**.

The propanone causes skin dryness, so the student should wear gloves/use forceps to handle the chromatogram **(1)**.

29. Drinking water

1 A **(1)**

2 (a) to sterilise the water/to kill microbes **(1)**

(b) The concentration of chlorine is high enough to kill microbes **(1)** but low enough so that it is not harmful to people **(1)**.

3 sedimentation **(1)** to remove larger insoluble particles **(1)**

filtration **(1)** to remove smaller insoluble particles **(1)**

4 Unlike tap water, distilled water does not contain dissolved salts **(1)**. These would interfere with the analysis/react with test substances/give a false-positive result **(1)**.

5 (a) (simple) distillation **(1)**

(b) A lot of energy is needed/a lot of fuel is needed to boil the water. **(1)**

6 $Al_2(SO_4)_3(aq) + 6H_2O(l) \rightarrow 2Al(OH)_3(s) + 3H_2SO_4(aq)$ **(1)**

30. Extended response – Separating mixtures

The answer may include some of the following points: **(6)**

physical states:

- Substance A is solid; substances B and C are liquids.

separating A from B and C:

- Substance **A** is insoluble in **B** and **C**.
- so it cannot be separated by paper chromatography
- but it can be separated from **B** and **C** by filtration.
- Substance **A** collects as a residue in the filter paper.
- It can be washed with **B** or **C** on the filter paper
- then dried in a warm oven
- below 115 °C to stop it melting.

separating **B** and **C**:

- (After filtration) the filtrate is a mixture of substances **B** and **C**.

- They have different boiling points
- so they can be separated by *fractional* distillation.
- Substance **B** has the lower boiling point.
- Substance **B** distils off first (and can be collected).
- Continue heating to leave substance **C** in the flask.
- Stop heating when the temperature starts to rise.

31. Acids and alkalis

1 D **(1)**

2 (a) The green colour means that the indicator is neutral **(1)**, so the pH is 7 **(1)**.

(b) red/orange **(1)**

3 (a) $2Mg + O_2 \rightarrow 2MgO$ **(1)**

(b) It is alkaline/contains an alkali/has a pH greater than 7. **(1)**

4 1 mark for each correct row to 4 marks maximum:

Formula of substance	Type of substance	
	Acid	Alkali
NaOH		✓
HCl	✓	
H_2SO_4	✓	
NH_3		✓

5 (a) litmus: blue, red **(1)**; phenolphthalein: pink, colourless **(1)**

(b) purple **(1)**

32. Bases and alkalis

1 B **(1)**

2 (a) sodium nitrate **(1)**

(b) sodium carbonate + nitric acid = sodium nitrate + water + carbon dioxide **(1)**

(c) bubbles **(1)**; powder disappears/dissolves/colourless solution forms **(1)**

3 (a) calcium chloride solution **(1)**

(b) hydrogen **(1)**

4 (a) (Bubble the gas through) limewater **(1)** which turns milky/cloudy white **(1)**.

(b) *Lighted* splint (ignites the gas) **(1)** with a (squeaky) pop **(1)**.

5 (a) A base is any substance that reacts with an acid **(1)** to form a salt and water only **(1)**.

(b) alkali **(1)**

(c) zinc sulfate **(1)**

33. Neutralisation

1 Hydrogen ions, H^+, from the acid **(1)** react with hydroxide/OH^- ions from the alkali **(1)** to form water **(1)**.

2 (a) $CaO + 2HCl \rightarrow CaCl_2 + H_2O$ **(1)**

(b) $Ca(OH)_2 + 2HCl \rightarrow CaCl_2 + 2H_2O$

1 mark for formulae, 1 mark for balancing

3 points plotted accurately ($\pm \frac{1}{2}$ square) **(1)**; line of best fit **(1)**

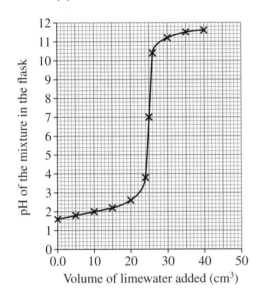

34. Salts from insoluble bases

1 (a) to react with *all* the acid **(1)** so that only a salt and water are left (with an excess of solid) **(1)**

(b) to make the reaction happen faster/to increase the rate of reaction **(1)**

(c) filtration/filtering **(1)**

(d) crystallisation/evaporation **(1)**

2 (a) measuring cylinder/pipette/burette **(1)**

(b) two improvements with reasons: 1 mark for improvement, 1 mark for its reason(s), e.g.

- Stir, to mix the reactants.

- Add copper oxide one spatula at a time, to reduce waste.

- Warm the acid first, to make the reaction happen faster.

(c) Filter **(1)** to stop excess copper oxide contaminating the solution/crystals **(1)**.

35. Salts from soluble bases

1 C **(1)**

2 top label: burette **(1)**; bottom label: (conical) flask **(1)**

3 (a) hydrochloric acid **(1)**

(b) (volumetric) pipette **(1)**

(c) pink to colourless **(1)** *Both colours needed in the correct order for the mark.*

(d) (i) to get an idea of how much acid must be added **(1)**

(ii) run 1: 24.90; run 2: 24.40; run 3: 24.50 **(1)**

(iii) 24.90 cm³ **(1)**

(iv) (24.40 + 24.50)/2 = 24.45 cm³ **(1)**

(e) Repeat the titration without the indicator **(1)** using the mean titre volume of hydrochloric acid **(1)**.

36. Making insoluble salts

1 B **(1)**

2 D **(1)**

3 (a) calcium nitrate/calcium chloride **(1)** with sodium hydroxide/potassium hydroxide/ ammonium hydroxide **(1)**

(b) Answer depends on the combination used in part (**a**), e.g. sodium nitrate/potassium nitrate/ammonium nitrate (if calcium nitrate used); sodium chloride/potassium chloride/ ammonium chloride (if calcium chloride used). **(1)**

(c) The reaction is already very fast/the precipitate forms very quickly/the reaction has a low activation energy. **(1)**

4 (a) $Na_2CO_3(aq) + CaCl_2(aq) \rightarrow 2NaCl(aq) + CaCO_3(s)$

1 mark for balancing, 1 mark for correct state symbols

(b) Add water to dissolve each solid separately/ sodium carbonate and calcium chloride **(1)** then mix. Separate the precipitate of calcium carbonate using filtration **(1)**. Wash the precipitate using water (e.g. on the filter paper), **(1)**, then dry it by putting it in a warm oven/between pieces of filter paper **(1)**.

37. Extended response – Making salts

The answer may include some of the following points: **(6)**

the titration:

- Rinse a burette with dilute hydrochloric acid, then fill the burette with the acid.
- Measure 25 cm³ of sodium hydroxide solution using a pipette
- into a conical flask.
- conical flask on a white tile
- Add a few drops of phenolphthalein/methyl orange indicator.
- Record the start reading on the burette.
- Add dilute hydrochloric acid from the burette to the sodium hydroxide solution.
- Swirl the flask.
- Rinse the inside of the flask during titration using distilled water.
- Add drop by drop near the end-point.
- Stop when colour changes/pink to colourless (phenolphthalein)/yellow to orange (methyl orange).
- Record the end reading on the burette.
- Repeat the experiment
- until consistent/concordant results are obtained.

using the titre:

- Add 25 cm³ of sodium hydroxide to the flask.
- Do not add indicator.
- Add the titre/mean titre volume of dilute hydrochloric acid from the burette.

producing the crystals:

- Pour the mixture into an evaporating basin.
- Heat over a hot water bath
- until most of the water has evaporated.
- Allow to cool and pour away excess water.
- Dry crystals between filter paper/in a warm oven.

38. Electrolysis

1 D **(1)**

2 1 mark for each correct row to 4 marks maximum:

	Positively charged	Negatively charged
Anode	✓	
Anion		✓
Cathode		✓
Cation	✓	

3 An electrolyte is an ionic **(1)** compound in the molten/liquid state or dissolved in water **(1)**.

4 bromine **(1)** *not bromide*

5 the negatively charged electrode, because sodium ions are positively charged/opposite charges attract **(1)** *Electrode and reason must be correct for the mark.*

6 MnO_4^- ions/manganate(VII) ions **(1)** move to the positively charged electrode/oppositely charged electrode **(1)**.

39. Electrolysing solutions

1 (a) B **(1)**

(b) D **(1)**

(c) copper **(1)**

2 (a) Na^+, Cl^- **(1)** H^+, OH^- **(1)**

(b) (i) chlorine **(1)**

(ii) hydrogen **(1)**

3 anode – oxygen **(1)**, cathode – hydrogen **(1)**

4 hydroxide/OH^- **(1)**

40. Investigating electrolysis

1 (a) inert **(1)**

(b) anode because it is positively charged **(1)** and oxygen is formed from negatively charged ions/hydroxide ions **(1)**

2 (a) time **(1)**

(b) gain in mass by copper cathode **(1)**

(c) non-inert because the anode loses mass/the cathode gains mass/the electrodes change in mass **(1)**

(d) change on the y-axis $= 0.15 - 0.04 = 0.11$

change on the x-axis $= 0.8 - 0.2 = 0.6$ **(1)**

gradient $= 0.11/0.6$ **(1)**

$= 0.18$ g/A **(1)**

41. Extended response – Electrolysis

The answer may include some of the following points: **(6)**

solid copper chloride powder:

- Its ions are not free to move
- in the solid state
- so there are no visible changes
- so the solid powder does not conduct.

copper chloride solution:

- Its ions are free to move
- when dissolved in water/in solution
- so the solution does conduct.
- Brown solid is copper.
- Yellow–green gas is chlorine.

electrode reactions:

- positively charged ions/copper ions attracted to negative electrode/cathode
- negatively charged ions/chloride ions attracted to positive electrode/anode
- overall reaction: $CuCl_2(aq) \rightarrow Cu(s) + Cl_2(g)$.

42. The reactivity series

1 (a) D **(1)**

(b) two from the following, for 1 mark each: starting temperature (of water/acid); mass of metal; surface area of metal; amount/moles of metal

2 named metal that is less reactive than hydrogen, e.g. silver/copper/gold/platinum **(1)**

3 (a) (i) hydrogen **(1)**

(ii) *Lighted* splint ignites the gas **(1)** with a (squeaky) pop **(1)**.

(b) magnesium oxide **(1)**

4 (a) $Al_2O_3(s) + 3H_2SO_4(aq) \rightarrow Al_2(SO_4)_3(aq) + 3H_2O(l)$ **(1)**

(b) To begin with, the acid reacts with the aluminium oxide layer **(1)** but once this has gone, it reacts with the aluminium **(1)**.

43. Metal displacement reactions

1 (a) Copper is more reactive than silver **(1)**.

(b) $Cu(s) + 2AgNO_3(aq) \rightarrow 2Ag(s) + Cu(NO_3)_2(aq)$

1 mark for balancing, 1 mark for state symbols

2 (a) copper **(1)**

(b) A metal cannot displace itself. **(1)**

(c) (i) magnesium > metal X **(1)**

(ii) 1 mark for experiment, 1 mark for expected result, e.g. Put a piece of zinc into copper nitrate solution – if zinc is more reactive it gets coated/if zinc is less reactive there is no visible change **OR** put a piece of copper in zinc nitrate – if copper is more reactive it gets coated/if copper is less reactive there is no visible change.

3 Aluminium is more reactive than iron **(1)** because aluminium can displace iron from its compounds/from iron oxide **(1)**.

44. Explaining metal reactivity

1 A cation is a positively charged ion. **(1)**

2 (a) Ca^{2+} **(1)**

(b) Two **(1)** electrons are lost from the outer shell **(1)**.

(c) (i) potassium **(1)**

(ii) gold **(1)**

(d) copper/silver/gold **(1)**

3 Zinc is more reactive than copper **(1)** because it forms cations more easily/it loses electrons more easily **(1)**.

45. Metal ores

1 C **(1)**

2 (a) A **(1)**

(b) Hydrogen is flammable/could explode. **(1)**

3 a rock or mineral that contains enough metal/metal compound **(1)** to make its extraction worthwhile/economical **(1)**

4 (a) tin oxide + carbon → tin **(1)** + carbon monoxide/carbon dioxide **(1)**

(b) Carbon is oxidised **(1)** because it gains oxygen **(1)**.

5 (a) Oil keeps air/oxygen away from the sodium. **(1)**

(b) Copper is unreactive/low down on the reactivity series. **(1)**

46. Iron and aluminium

1 (a) sodium/calcium/magnesium **(1)**

(b) lead/copper **(1)**

2 (a) iron oxide + carbon → iron **(1)** + carbon monoxide/carbon dioxide **(1)**

(b) Carbon is more reactive than iron/iron is less reactive than carbon. **(1)**

(c) Iron oxide is reduced, because it loses oxygen. **(1)**

3 (a) A lot of electricity is needed/electricity is more expensive than carbon. **(1)**

(b) (i) aluminium **(1)**

(ii) oxygen **(1)**

(c) The carbon reacts with the oxygen formed/ the electrodes burn away. **(1)**

4 Zinc is most likely to be extracted by heating zinc oxide with carbon **(1)** because zinc is less reactive than carbon/carbon is more reactive than zinc/electrolysis is more expensive than heating with carbon **(1)**.

47. Recycling metals

1 one mark for each correct row to 2 marks:

Feature of recycling metals	Disadvantage (✓)
Used metal items must be collected.	✓
The use of finite resources is decreased.	
Different metals must be sorted.	✓
Metals can be melted down.	

Deduct 1 mark for each extra row completed.

2 two of the following, for 1 mark each: dust produced; noisy; land used; wildlife loses habitat; extra traffic; landscape destroyed

3 (a) Most lead for recycling is found in batteries **(1)** so lead does not need to be sorted from scrap metal waste **(1)**.

(b) two of the following, for 1 mark each: conserves metal ores/limited resources; less energy needed; fewer quarries needed/saves land/landscape; less noise/dust produced

4 (a) aluminium **(1)**

(b) Steel and aluminium are much more abundant than tin in the Earth's crust **(1)**; tin is much more valuable than steel or aluminium **(1)**. *Accept the reverse arguments.*

48. Life-cycle assessments

1 2, 1, 4, 3 **(1)**

2 (a) (i) energy = $16.5 \times 0.24 = 3.96$ MJ **(1)**

(ii) $16.5 \times 0.20 = 3.3$ MJ **(1)**

(b) difference in mass between bottles in 1996 and 2016 = 0.24 − 0.20

= 0.04 kg **(1)**

difference in mass of CO_2 emitted = $0.04 \times 1.2 = 0.048$ kg **(1)**

3 (a) PVC: producing the material; wooden: transport and installation **(1)**

(b) the PVC frame **(1)** because it uses less energy/20% of the energy/five times less energy **(1)**

49. Extended response – Reactivity of metals

The answer may include some of the following points: **(6)**

basic method:

- I would start with powdered copper, iron, zinc, copper oxide, iron oxide and zinc oxide.

- Mix a spatula of a metal powder with a spatula of a metal oxide powder.

- Put the mixture in a steel lid.

- Heat strongly from below.

- Record observations.

- Repeat with a different combination of metal and metal oxide.

Expected results (in writing and/or as a table, as here):

	Copper oxide	Iron oxide	Zinc oxide
Copper	not done	no visible change	no visible change
Iron	reaction seen/brown coating	not done	no visible change
Zinc	reaction seen/brown coating	reaction seen/black coating	not done

using the results:

- Count the number of reactions seen for each metal.

- Zinc has two reactions; iron has one reaction; copper has no reactions.

- order of reactivity (most reactive first): zinc, iron, copper

controlling risks:

- Use tongs because substances/apparatus/steel lid is hot.

- Wear eye protection to avoid contact with (hot) powders.
- Stand back/use a safety screen/fume cupboard to avoid breathing in escaping substances/to avoid skin contact with hot powders.

50. Transition metals

1 C **(1)**

2 between groups 2 and 3 **(1)** in the central/middle/centre **(1)** part of the periodic table

3 (a) **B** *and* **D (1)**

 (b) Transition metals form coloured compounds. **(1)**

4 (a) metal **B (1)**

 (b) Transition metals (typically) have high melting points. **(1)**

5 (a) catalyst **(1)**

 (b) Osmium is a transition metal (and these show catalytic activity). **(1)**

51. Rusting

1 D **(1)**

2 (a) oxygen/air **(1)**, water **(1)**

 (b) hydrated iron oxide/(III) oxide **(1)**

3 (a) The layer of oil stops air/oxygen **(1)** and water reaching the steel **(1)**.

 (b) (i) The crystals absorb water **(1)**; steel cannot rust unless water is present **(1)**.

 (ii) The paint would stop the parts moving/the paint would rub off in use **(1)**.

4 to improve their appearance **(1)**

5 (a) sacrificial protection **(1)**

 (b) Zinc is more reactive than iron **(1)** so zinc oxidises instead of the iron/before the iron does **(1)**.

52. Alloys

1 C **(1)**

2 two from the following, for 1 mark each: It is unreactive; It does not corrode/tarnish; it is malleable/shaped easily; it is shiny.

3 one of the following for 1 mark: Alloy steels are stronger/harder/resist corrosion better.

4 Aluminium is stronger than copper **(1)** and its density is lower so the cables will be more lightweight **(1)**. *Both metals have good corrosion resistance so this is not a factor for choosing aluminium rather than copper.*

5 The layers of atoms in aluminium can slide over each other easily **(1)**. Magnesium atoms are larger/distort the layered structure **(1)** so the layers in the alloy cannot slide over each other so easily **(1)**.

53. Extended response – Alloys and corrosion

The answer may include some of the following points: **(6)**

method:

- electrolyte of silver nitrate solution/$AgNO_3$(aq)
- as all nitrates are soluble in water
- Put the spoon and a piece of (pure) silver in the electrolyte.
- Use a DC/direct current power supply.
- Connect the spoon to the negative terminal of the power supply.
- Connect the silver to the positive terminal of the power supply.
- The spoon is the cathode.
- Pure silver is the anode.
- Turn on the power supply.
- Allow time for the silver layer to form.
- Remove the spoon.
- Wash the electroplated spoon to remove electrolyte/silver nitrate solution.

These points could be made using a suitably labelled or annotated diagram instead.

54. Accurate titrations

1 gradual change in colour/no sharp end-point **(1)**

2 (a) phenolphthalein/methyl orange/litmus **(1)**

 (b) Colour change matches the indicator given in part (**a**) for 1 mark:

 phenolphthalein: pink to colourless *not clear*; methyl orange: yellow to orange–red; litmus: blue to red

3 The accurate apparatus needed is a pipette/volumetric pipette **(1)**. To use it accurately, I would read at eye level/draw the liquid up to the line/bottom of the meniscus on the line **(1)**. The safety apparatus needed is a pipette filler **(1)**.

4 (a) start reading: 0.80 cm^3 **(1)**; end-point reading: 25.25 cm^3 **(1)**

 (b) titre = (end-point reading) – (start reading) = 25.25 – 0.80 = 24.45 cm^3 **(1)**

5 (a) to make sure that acid reacts completely with the alkali **(1)**

(b) to obtain an accurate end-point/to avoid going past the end-point **(1)**

(c) to obtain an accurate reading/to avoid a parallax error **(1)**

55. Percentage yield

1 B **(1)**

2 the maximum mass of product for a given mass of limiting reactant/calculated from the balanced equation **(1)**

3 (a) The reaction might not be complete/go to completion **(1)** and some magnesium oxide could be lost during the experiment **(1)**.

(b) $(3.0/4.0) \times 100$ **(1)**

= 75% **(1)**

4 (a) $(2.43/2.86) \times 100$ **(1)**

= 85% **(1)**

(b) $(70/100) \times 50$ **(1)**

= 35 g **(1)**

56. Atom economy

1 A **(1)**

2 total M_r of desired product, KNO_3 = 101

total M_r of all products = 101 + 18 = 119 **(1)**

atom economy = $(101/119) \times 100$ = 84.9% **(1)**

3 total M_r of desired product, Fe
= 2 × 56 = 112

total M_r of all products
= (2 × 56) + (3 × 28) = 196 **(1)**

atom economy = $(112/196) \times 100$ = 57.1% **(1)**

4 M_r of C_2H_5OH = (2 × 12) + (6 × 1) + 16 = 46 *and*

M_r of CO_2 = 12 + (2 × 16) = 44 **(1)**

total M_r of desired product = (2 × 46) = 92

total M_r of all
products = (2 × 46) + (2 × 44) = 180 **(1)**

atom economy = $(92/180) \times 100$ = 51.1% **(1)**

57. Exam skills – Chemical calculations

1 (a) (i) M_r of BaO = 137 + 16 = 153 **(1)**

(ii) M_r of O_2 = (2 × 16) = 32 **(1)**

(b) 153 g of BaO reacts with 32 g of O_2.

1 g of BaO reacts with 32/153 = 0.209 g of O_2. **(1)**

250 g of BaO reacts with 250 × 0.209 = 52.3 g of O_2 (to 3 significant figures). **(1)**

(c) There is only one product/all the reactant atoms end up in the desired product. **(1)**

(d) M_r of BaO = 153 and M_r of O_2 = 32

total M_r of all products =
(2 × 153) + 32 = 338 **(1)**

atom economy = $(32/338) \times 100$ = 9.5% **(1)**

(e) (i) The reaction may be incomplete (at stage 1 and/or at stage 2)/some solid or gas may be lost when handled. **(1)**

(ii) percentage yield
= $(21.0/24.7) \times 100$ = 85.0% **(1)**

(f) concentration = 21.3/2.50 **(1)**

= 8.52 g dm^{-3} **(1)**

58. The Haber process

1 (a) D **(1)**

(b) The reaction is reversible. **(1)**

2 (a) temperature 450 °C **(1)**; pressure: 200 atmospheres/20 MPa **(1)**

(b) It is a catalyst **(1)**; it makes the reaction happen faster **(1)**.

3 (a) none/no visible change **(1)**

(b) (i) The rate of the forward and backward reactions is the same/equal **(1)** and they continue to happen **(1)**.

(ii) They do not change/they remain constant. **(1)**

59. Making fertilisers

1 1 mark for each correct row to 3 marks maximum (*NH_4NO_3 already completed*):

Fertiliser compound	Element required by plants		
	Potassium	Phosphorus	Nitrogen
NH_4NO_3			✓
$(NH_4)_2SO_4$			✓
K_3PO_4	✓	✓	
KNO_3	✓		✓

2 neutralisation **(1)**

3 (a) Titration lets you find the correct proportions of acid and alkali **(1)**

to mix together so that the solution contains only salt and water **(1)**.

(b) Heat the solution gently to evaporate some of the water **(1)**; allow to cool so crystals form **(1)**; pour away excess water/remove crystals from the dish **(1)**; dry with filter paper/dry in a warm oven **(1)**.

4   1 mark for each correct row to a maximum of 4 marks:

Feature	Laboratory	Industrial
ammonia and sulfuric acid manufactured from their raw materials		✓
ammonia and sulfuric acid bought from manufacturers	✓	
small-scale production	✓	
continuous production		✓

60. Fuel cells

1   B **(1)**

2   A fuel cell produces a constant voltage for as long as it is supplied with air/oxygen *or* fuel/hydrogen **(1)** and fuel/hydrogen *or* air/oxygen **(1)**.

3   (a) water **(1)**

(b) Air contains oxygen/it supplies oxygen **(1)** which reacts with the hydrogen/fuel **(1)**.

4   (a) There are many more charging points/ electric sockets **(1)** so the distance between them is less/can recharge at home/can recharge at work or at home **(1)**.

(b) advantage for 1 mark, and 1 mark for reason, e.g.

- The car does not need to store hydrogen in a tank, which is safer.

- The metal hydride powder is solid, so it is easier/safer to store than hydrogen.

- Water is a liquid, which is easier to store than hydrogen.

- The car may have a greater range because it may need refuelling less often.

61. The alkali metals

1   C **(1)**

2   table completed, e.g.

Alkali metal	Flame colour	Description
lithium	does not ignite	fizzes steadily disappears slowly
sodium	orange if ignited	fizzes rapidly **(1)** melts to form a ball/disappears quickly **(1)**
potassium	lilac **(1)**	fizzes very rapidly/gives off sparks **(1)** disappears very quickly/explodes at the end **(1)**

3   $2Na(s) + 2H_2O(l) \rightarrow 2NaOH(aq) + H_2(g)$

1 mark for balancing, 1 mark for state symbols

4   Their atoms all have one electron in their outer shell. **(1)**

5   They are very reactive/react with water/react with air **(1)**; oil keeps water away/air away **(1)**.

6   (a) FrOH **(1)**

(b) Idea of a violent reaction, e.g. violent fizzing/explosion/flame/metal disappears almost immediately. **(1)**

7   Going down the Group, the size of the atoms increases **(1)**. The outer electron becomes further from the nucleus/more shielded **(1)** so the outer electron is lost more easily **(1)**.

62. The halogens

1   B **(1)**

2   Their atoms all have seven electrons in their outer shell. **(1)**

3   (a) chlorine: yellow–green **(1)** gas **(1)**; bromine: red–brown **(1)** liquid **(1)**

(b) very dark grey/black **(1)** solid **(1)**

4   (a) answer in the range 6000–7000 kg/m³ **(1)**

(b) Going down the Group, the density increases (and astatine is below iodine at 4933 kg/m³). **(1)**

5   (a) covalent **(1)**

(b) intermolecular forces **(1)**

63. Reactions of halogens

1   (a) $H_2 + Cl_2 \rightarrow 2HCl$ **(1)**

(b) C **(1)**

(c) Going down group 7, the elements become less reactive **(1)**. I can tell this because the energy needed for them to start reacting increases (going down the group/from fluorine to chlorine to bromine) **(1)**.

2 (a) sodium + chlorine → sodium chloride **(1)**

(b) $FeCl_3$ **(1)**

(c) (i) iron(II) ion: Fe^{2+} **(1)**; iodide ion: I^- **(1)**

(ii) $Fe + I_2 \rightarrow FeI_2$

1 mark for correct formulae, 1 mark for balancing

3 Fluorine atoms are smaller **(1)** than chlorine atoms, so its outer shell is closer to the nucleus **(1)** and it gains an outer electron more easily **(1)**.

64. Halogen displacement reactions

1 (a) D **(1)**

(b) bromine + potassium iodide → iodine + potassium bromide **(1)**

2 (a) The order of reactivity, starting with the most reactive, is chlorine, bromine, iodine **(1)** because chlorine displaces bromine from bromide and iodine from iodide **(1)** but bromine displaces only iodine from iodide. Iodine cannot displace chlorine or bromine **(1)**.

(b) A halogen cannot displace itself (so no reaction will be seen). **(1)**

(c) Iodine is more reactive than astatine/astatine is less reactive than iodine **(1)** and a more reactive halogen will displace a less reactive halogen **(1)**.

3 (a) $2F_2(g) + 2H_2O(l) \rightarrow 4HF(aq) + O_2(g)$ **(1)**

(b) Fluorine reacts with water/does not form a solution of fluorine. **(1)**

(c) Chlorine is a pale (yellow–green) gas. **(1)**

65. The noble gases

1 A **(1)**

2 Balloons and airships rise because helium is less dense than air/has a low density. **(1)**

Helium is inert, so it will not catch fire. **(1)**

3 (a) helium **(1)**

(b) density increases down the Group **(1)**

(c) answer in the range −40 °C to −20 °C **(1)**; melting point increases down the group **(1)**

4 The outer shells of their atoms are full/complete **(1)** so they have no tendency to gain/lose/share electrons/to form ions/to form covalent bonds **(1)**.

66. Extended response – Groups

The answer may include some of the following points: **(6)**

reaction between sodium and chlorine:

- Sodium atoms transfer electrons
- from their outer shell
- to the outer shell of chlorine atoms.
- Each sodium atom loses one electron
- to form an Na^+ ion.
- Each chlorine atom gains one electron
- to form a Cl^- ion.
- Oppositely charged ions/Na^+ ions and Cl^- ions attract each other.
- Ionic bonds form.
- diagram showing the electronic configuration of Na, e.g. 2.8.1
- diagram showing the electronic configuration of Na^+, e.g. 2.8 with + charge indicated
- diagram showing the electronic configuration of Cl, e.g. 2.8.7
- diagram showing the electronic configuration of Cl^-, e.g. 2.8 with − charge indicated.

violence of reaction between caesium and fluorine:

- Reactivity increases down group 1/Cs loses its electrons more easily (than Li, Na, K, Rb).
- Reactivity decreases down group 7/F gains electrons more easily (than any other group 7 element).
- Caesium and fluorine are most reactive/very reactive.

67. Rates of reaction

1 B **(1)**

2 1 mark for each correct row:

Change in reaction conditions	Frequency of collisions increased	Energy of collisions increased
increased concentration of a reacting solution	✓	
increased pressure of reacting a gas	✓	
increased temperature of reaction mixture	✓	✓

3 (a) It increases. **(1)**

(b) The powder has a larger *surface area:volume ratio* **(1)** so there are more frequent collisions between reactant particles **(1)**. *Not 'there are more collisions'.*

4 (a) a substance that speeds up a reaction without altering the products **(1)** and is unchanged chemically **(1)** and is also unchanged in mass **(1)** (at the end of the reaction)

The answers 'chemically' and 'mass' can be in either order.

(b) A catalyst provides an alternative pathway **(1)** with a lower activation energy **(1)**.

(c) (i) enzyme **(1)**

(ii) making alcoholic drinks/wine/beer **(1)**

68. Investigating rates

1 (a) Collect the gas in a gas syringe/upturned burette of water/upturned measuring cylinder of water. **(1)**

(b) The sulfur dioxide will dissolve in the water **(1)** so most will not escape/the volume measurement will be too low **(1)**.

(c) Sodium chloride solution and water are both clear and colourless **(1)** so you could not tell that they are being produced **(1)**.

2 (a) total volume of liquid is kept the same **(1)**; concentration of dilute hydrochloric acid is kept the same **(1)**

(b) 8 **(1)**, 24, 40 **(1)**

(c) As the concentration increases the rate increases/rate is proportional to concentration **(1)**; when the concentration increases three times the rate increases three times/when the concentration increases five times the rate increases five times **(1)**.
Or Rate is *directly* proportional to the concentration. **(2)**

69. Exam skills – Rates of reaction

1 (a) all points plotted correctly ± ½ square **(2)**

1 mark if one error

single line of best fit passing through all the points **(1)**

Do not use a ruler to join the points (apart from the last two) because a curve is required here.

(b) time taken: 100 s **(1)**

Explanation: the mass does not change any more/the line becomes horizontal. **(1)** *not 'straight'*

(c) line drawn to the left of the original line **(1)** becoming horizontal at 0.96 g **(1)**

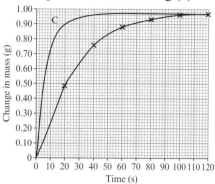

70. Heat energy changes

1 In an exothermic change or reaction, heat energy is given out **(1)** but, in an endothermic change or reaction, heat energy is taken in **(1)**.

2 C **(1)**

3 (a) endothermic **(1)**

(b) acid-alkali neutralisation **(1)**; aqueous displacement **(1)**

4 (a) Measure the temperature of the acid before and after adding magnesium **(1)** using a thermometer **(1)** and the temperature should increase **(1)**.

(b) $Mg(s) + 2HCl(aq) \rightarrow MgCl_2(aq) + H_2(g)$

1 mark for balancing, 1 mark for state symbols

(c) More heat energy **(1)** is released when bonds form in the products **(1)** than is needed to break bonds in the reactants **(1)**.

71. Reaction profiles

1 activation energy **(1)**

2 There is more stored energy in the reactants than in the products **(1)** so, during the reaction, energy is given out **(1)**.

3 diagram completed with upwards arch between reactants and product lines **(1)**; activation energy correctly identified **(1)**

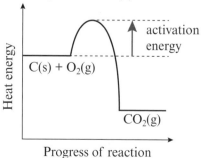

4 activation energy correctly identified **(1)**; overall energy change correctly identified **(1)**

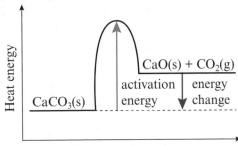

72. Crude oil

1 (a) D **(1)**

(b) D **(1)**

(c) It is no longer being made/it is made extremely slowly. **(1)**

2 (a) C_6H_{12} **(1)**

(b) They are compounds of hydrogen and carbon **(1)** only **(1)**.

3 (a) petrol/diesel oil/kerosene/fuel oil **(1)**

(b) a starting material **(1)** for an industrial chemical process **(1)**

73. Fractional distillation

1 (a) (i) gases **(1)**

(ii) bitumen **(1)**

(iii) gases **(1)**

(iv) bitumen **(1)**

(b) (i) bitumen **(1)**

(ii) kerosene **(1)**

(c) petrol **(1)**, diesel oil **(1)**

2 alkanes **(1)**

3 Oil is heated so that it evaporates/boils/vaporises **(1)**. The vapours are passed into a column, which is hot at the bottom and cold at the top **(1)**.

Hydrocarbons rise, and condense **(1)** at different heights, depending on boiling point/size of molecules/strength of intermolecular forces **(1)**.

74. Alkanes

1 C **(1)**

2 A **(1)**

3 (a) C_2H_6 **(1)**

(b) Correct structure for 1 mark, e.g.

$$H-\overset{\overset{\displaystyle H}{|}}{\underset{\underset{\displaystyle H}{|}}{C}}-\overset{\overset{\displaystyle H}{|}}{\underset{\underset{\displaystyle H}{|}}{C}}-\overset{\overset{\displaystyle H}{|}}{\underset{\underset{\displaystyle H}{|}}{C}}-H$$

(c) Going from one alkane to the next, the molecular formula changes by CH_2/one carbon atom *and* two hydrogen atoms. **(1)**

4 (a) C_nH_{2n+2} **(1)**

(b) C_6H_{14} **(1)**

75. Incomplete combustion

1 (a) complete combustion **(1)**

(b) 1 mark for each correct column, e.g.

	Incomplete combustion	Complete combustion
Water	✓	✓
Carbon	✓	
Carbon monoxide	✓	
Carbon dioxide	✓	✓

2 flame **A** because incomplete combustion occurs **(1)** producing soot/carbon particles **(1)**

3 (a) They cause lung disease/bronchitis/make existing lung disease worse, e.g. asthma. **(1)**

(b) $C_6H_6 + 4O_2 \rightarrow 2C + 3CO + CO_2 + 3H_2O$ **(1)**

(c) When breathed in, carbon monoxide combines with haemoglobin/red blood cells **(1)** so less oxygen can be carried/there is a lack of oxygen to cells **(1)**.

76. Acid rain

1 (a) rain cloud **(1)**; acid rain **(1)**; power station **(1)**; acidic gases **(1)**; distant city **(1)**

(b) Sulfur (impurities) in the fuel **(1)** react with oxygen **(1)**.

2 Oxygen and nitrogen from the air **(1)** react together at the high temperatures inside the engine **(1)**.

3 (a) Marble/calcium carbonate reacts with acids/acidic rainwater **(1)** but granite does not **(1)**.

(b) damage to trees/plants/soil **(1)** makes lakes acidic/harms aquatic life **(1)**

77. Choosing fuels

1 (a) crude oil **(1)**

(b) Petrol is used as a fuel for cars. Kerosene is used as a fuel for aircraft **(1)** and diesel oil is used as a fuel for some cars/some trains **(1)**.

2 It is being used up faster than it can form. **(1)**

3 (a) $2H_2 + O_2 \rightarrow 2H_2O$ **(1)**

(b) carbon dioxide **(1)**

4 (a) (i) Petrol releases more energy per dm^3 than hydrogen does. **(1)**

(ii) Hydrogen releases more energy per kg than petrol does. **(1)**

(b) More liquid hydrogen can be stored in the same volume/same number of particles in the liquid can be stored in a smaller volume. **(1)**

78. Cracking

1 (a) alkene/unsaturated **(1)**

(b) $C_{10}H_{22} \rightarrow C_8H_{18} + C_2H_4$

1 mark for correct reactant, 1 mark for correct products

2 D **(1)**

3 (a) It is a catalyst. **(1)**

(b) a reaction in which larger alkanes are broken down into smaller (more useful) alkanes/smaller (more useful) saturated hydrocarbons **(1)** and smaller alkenes/unsaturated hydrocarbons **(1)**

4 Smaller hydrocarbons are in higher demand/more useful **(1)**. Cracking helps to match supply with demand **(1)**.

79. Extended response – Fuels

The answer may include some of the following points: **(6)**

why incomplete combustion happens:

● Incomplete combustion happens when there is insufficient oxygen/air.

● This can happen if there is not enough ventilation, such as inside a tent.

● Not enough oxygen for complete combustion.

products and their problems:

● carbon monoxide gas produced

● Carbon monoxide is toxic.

● Carbon monoxide is colourless/odourless so it may not be noticed.

● combines with haemoglobin/red blood cells

● so less oxygen can be carried/there is a lack of oxygen to cells

● can cause unconsciousness/death

● carbon particles/soot produced

● cause lung disease/bronchitis/make existing lung disease worse

● cause blackening, e.g. of the bottom of the kettle/the inside of the tent

● balanced equation, e.g.
$C_3H_8 + 3O_2 \rightarrow 4H_2O + 2CO + C$. *Many*

incomplete combustion reactions and their equations are possible.

other problems:

● Less energy is released by incomplete combustion.

80. The early atmosphere

1 B **(1)**

2 (a) 10% **(1)**

(b) Water vapour (in the atmosphere) **(1)** condensed (and fell as rain) **(1)**.

(c) Carbon dioxide dissolved **(1)** in the oceans/water **(1)**.

3 (a) A *glowing* splint **(1)** relights **(1)**.

(b) The growth of primitive plants used carbon dioxide **(1)** and released oxygen **(1)** by the process of photosynthesis **(1)**.

81. Greenhouse effect

1 B **(1)**

2 correct order (top to bottom of the table): 2, 4, 1, 3

1 mark for one correct number (1, 2 or 3); 2 marks for all three numbers correct (1, 2 and 3)

3 (a) methane **(1)**

(b) Fossil fuels contain hydrocarbons/carbon **(1)**, which react with oxygen in the air to produce carbon dioxide **(1)**.

4 (a) It increases. **(1)**

(b) a worldwide increase **(1)** in temperatures **(1)**

(c) two from the following, for 1 mark each: climate change/change in global weather patterns/ice caps melting/sea levels rise/loss of habitats

82. Extended response – Atmospheric science

The answer may include some of the following points: **(6)**

Greenhouse effect:

● Carbon dioxide and some other gases in the atmosphere absorb heat energy

● radiated from the Earth

● then release energy

● which keeps the Earth warm.

processes releasing carbon dioxide:

● burning fossil fuels

● respiration

- volcanic activity.

processes absorbing carbon dioxide:

- dissolving in seawater

- photosynthesis.

discussing the data:

- As the concentration of carbon dioxide rises

- the mean global temperature rises.

- Human activity, e.g. burning fossil fuels, could cause an increase in temperature

- but there are some years when the temperature decreases, e.g. in the late 1940s.

- Carbon dioxide is also produced by other processes, e.g. by volcanic activity

- so it might not all be due to human activity.

- There might be a common factor not shown in the graphs that is responsible for both changes.

83. Tests for metal ions

1 1 mark for each correct flame colour, to 4 marks (*calcium already completed*):

copper, blue–green **(1)**; lithium, red **(1)**; potassium, lilac **(1)**; sodium, yellow **(1)**

2 (a) to make sure that there are no other substances that may produce a flame colour. **(1)**

(b) It would be difficult to see the flame test colour/the flame may not be hot enough/the sample or loop may not get hot enough. **(1)**

3 (a) blue **(1)**

(b) Iron(II) sulfate forms a green precipitate **(1)**; iron(III) sulfate forms a brown precipitate **(1)**.

(c) I would add more sodium hydroxide solution to white precipitate.

Aluminium hydroxide dissolves/forms a colourless solution **(1)** but calcium hydroxide does not **(1)**.

84. More tests for ions

1 (a) 1 mark for each correct colour, to 3 marks:

bromide, cream **(1)**; chloride, white **(1)**; iodide, yellow **(1)**

(b) Hydrochloric acid contains chloride **(1)** ions, which would react with silver ions to form a white precipitate (of silver chloride) **(1)**.

2 (a) bubbling/bubbles of gas **(1)**

(b) Pass the gas through limewater **(1)**, which should turn milky/cloudy white **(1)**.

3 (a) barium sulfate **(1)**

(b) The hydrochloric acid reacts with any carbonate **(1)** ions, so they cannot also give a white precipitate **(1)**.

4 (a) ammonia **(1)** *not 'ammonium'*

(b) Damp red **(1)** litmus paper turns blue **(1)**.

85. Instrumental methods

1 two from the following for 1 mark each: improved sensitivity/improved accuracy/ increased speed

2 (a) (i) The lithium spectrum has two lines **(1)** that are not present in the mix spectrum **(1)**.

(ii) Na^+ **(1)**; K^+ **(1)**

Answers can be in the other order.

(b) Obtain the reference spectra for different ions, then compare them with the spectrum from the unknown solution **(1)**. If the lines match/are the same, the ion must be the same **(1)**.

3 (a) 0.18 g dm^{-3} **(1)**

(b) 30% **(1)**

86. Extended response – Tests for ions

The answer may include some of the following points: **(6)**

test for carbonate ions:

- Add dilute acid to each sample.

- Lithium carbonate is the only one to produce bubbles.

- Confirm that bubbles are carbon dioxide using limewater.

- Limewater turns milky/cloudy white.

test for sulfate ions:

- Dissolve a little of each substance in water.

- Add a few drops of hydrochloric acid

- to prevent carbonate ions giving a white precipitate/false-positive result.

- Lithium carbonate solution should give brief bubbling.

- Add a few drops of barium chloride solution.

- White precipitate forms with ammonium sulfate solution, sodium sulfate solution, aluminium sulfate solution.

flame tests:

- Carry out a flame test on each solid.

- Lithium carbonate gives a red flame.

- Sodium sulfate gives a yellow flame.

hydroxide precipitate tests:

- Dissolve a little of each substance in water.

- Add a few drops of dilute sodium hydroxide solution.

- A white precipitate forms with aluminium sulfate solution.

- This redissolves/disappears to form a colourless solution on adding excess sodium hydroxide solution.

test for ammonium ions:

- Add a few drops of dilute sodium hydroxide solution to each solid/each solution.

- Warm gently

- ammonium sulfate releases ammonia gas

- which turns damp red litmus paper blue.

87. More about alkanes

1 (a) carbon dioxide **(1)** and water **(1)**

(b) $C_5H_{12} + 8O_2 \rightarrow 5CO_2 + 6H_2O$ **(1)**

(c) $C_{16}H_{34}$ **(1)**

2 (a) It is a compound of hydrogen and carbon **(1)** only **(1)**.

(b) Propane does not contain C=C bonds/ carbon–carbon double bonds **(1)**; it contains only C–C bonds/carbon–carbon single bonds **(1)**.

3 molecular formulae: CH_4 **(1)**; C_2H_6 **(1)**; structure **(1)**:

H—C—C—C—C—H (with H atoms shown around each C)

88. Alkenes

1 (a) It is a hydrocarbon because it is a compound of hydrogen and carbon **(1)** only.

It is unsaturated because it contains C=C/ carbon–carbon double **(1)** bonds.

(b) $C_2H_4 + 3O_2 \rightarrow 2CO_2 + 2H_2O$ **(1)**

(c) $C_{10}H_{20}$ **(1)**

2 Add bromine water (and shake); no colour change/stays orange with hexane **(1)**; turns from orange to colourless with hexene **(1)**.

3 Molecular formula: C_4H_8 **(1)**; Structure **(1)**:

H—C—C=C (with H atoms shown)

The H atom on the C–H group can be down as shown here, or up.

89. Addition polymers

1 C **(1)**

2 a substance of high average relative molecular mass/formula mass **(1)** made up of small repeating units **(1)**

3 (a) poly(ethene) **(1)**

(b) They have a C=C bond/carbon–carbon double bond **(1)**.

(c) addition polymerisation **(1)**

4 structure of propene **(1)**:

5 structure of repeating unit of poly(tetrafluoroethene) **(1)**:

90. Biological polymers

1 (a) four **(1)**

(b) nucleotides **(1)**

2 (a) amino acids **(1)**

(b) $C_2H_5NO_2$ **(1)**

3 (a) CH_2O **(1)**

(b) It contains atoms of carbon, hydrogen and oxygen. **(1)**

(c) sugars/simple sugars/monosaccharides **(1)**

91. Polymer problems

1 combustion – harmful gases produced **(1)**; burial in landfill – suitable sites running out **(1)**; break down by microbes – many polymers are non-biodegradable **(1)**; recycling – different polymers must be sorted **(1)**

Answers

2 (a) a hole in the ground, e.g. a disused quarry **(1)**, where waste is dumped and then covered over **(1)**

   (b) The polymers do not decompose, so the landfill sites fill up/become full. **(1)**

3 (a) (i) poly(ethene) + oxygen → carbon dioxide + water **(1)**

      (ii) environmental effect of increasing carbon dioxide in the atmosphere, e.g. global warming/climate change **(1)**

   (b) two from the following for 1 mark each: Volume/amount of waste is reduced; landfill sites do not fill up so quickly; energy released can be used, e.g. for heating or making electricity.

4 (a) The different polymers will need to be sorted from each other. **(1)**

   (b) Crude oil is conserved/less is used **(1)** because smaller amounts of new polymer are needed **(1)**.

92. Extended response – Hydrocarbons and polymers

The answer may include some of the following points: **(6)**

DNA:

• made from nucleotides

• four different nucleotides.

starch:

• made from sugars

• made from glucose.

proteins:

• made from amino acids

• about 20 different amino acids.

making poly(ethene):

• addition polymerisation

• ethene monomer needed

• One of the bonds in the C=C bond breaks.

• New C–C bond forms between monomers.

• (Many) ethene molecules join together to form poly(ethene).

• equation using drawn structures, e.g.

93. Alcohols

1 A **(1)**

2 (a) CH_3OH **(1)**

      structure of ethanol **(1)**, e.g.

   (b) O–H circled **(1)**

   (c) They contain the same functional group/the –OH group **(1)**; they have the same general formula/formula differs by CH_2 from one compound to the next **(1)**.

3 (a) bubbling/fizzing **(1)**; sodium dissolves/clear solution formed **(1)**

   (b) method **(1)** with correct observation **(1)**, e.g. Use a pH meter, pH >7; add universal indicator, blue/purple; add litmus, blue; add phenolphthalein, pink; add methyl orange, yellow.

   (c) $C_2H_5OH + 3O_2 \rightarrow 2CO_2 + 3H_2O$ **(1)**

94. Making ethanol

1 (a) C **(1)**

   (b) B **(1)**

   (c) (simple) sugars **(1)**

   (d) It provides enzymes. **(1)**

   (e) No oxygen is present/oxygen is kept out. **(1)**

2 (a) Their boiling points differ. **(1)**

   (b) Heat the dilute solution of ethanol using a Bunsen burner/electric heater **(1)**. Ethanol has a lower boiling point than water so it boils first **(1)**. Ethanol vapour travels to the condenser **(1)** where it is cooled and condensed to form a liquid **(1)**.

95. Carboxylic acids

1 named indicator **(1)** with appropriate colour **(1)**, e.g. universal indicator – yellow/orange; phenolphthalein – colourless; methyl orange – orange/red; litmus – red

2 (a) hydrogen **(1)**

   (b) bubbles given off **(1)**; sodium carbonate disappears/dissolves **(1)**

3 (a) O=C–O–H circled **(1)**

   (b) HCOOH **(1)**

   (c) correct structure of propanoic acid with all covalent bonds shown **(1)**

4 butanoic acid **(1)**

96. Investigating combustion

1 (a) a reaction in which heat energy is given out. **(1)**

(b) Use a shorter thermometer/clamp the thermometer to stop it falling over. **(1)**

(c) The fuel in the burner could spill then set alight. **(1)**

(d) one from the following, for 1 mark: distance of wick/flame to the can; size of flame; starting temperature of the water; change in temperature of the water; mass of fuel burned; heating time

2 (a) ethanol 24 °C **and** butanol 29 °C **(1)**

(b) ethanol: $(42 - 18)/0.40 = 60$ °C/g

butanol: $(47 - 18)/0.43 = 67$ °C/g **(1)**

So butanol produces the greatest change per gram of fuel **(1)**.

97. Nanoparticles

1 B **(1)**

2 (a) $10 \times 10 \times 6 = 600$ mm^2 **(1)**

(b) $10 \times 10 \times 10 = 1000$ mm^3 **(1)**

(c) $600/1000 = 0.6$ or 0.6:1 **(1)**

3 (a) The sunscreen containing nanoparticulate titanium dioxide is not visible on the skin. **(1)**

(b) (i) may be absorbed through broken skin/swallowed/could get into the food chain **(1)**

(ii) nanoparticles act as catalysts/may catalyse harmful reactions **(1)**

(c) Nanoparticles have a very large surface area:volume ratio **(1)** so reactant particles collide more frequently with the catalyst **(1)**.

98. Bulk materials

1 D **(1)**

2 (a) (i) copper **(1)**

(ii) zinc **(1)**

(b) It has the highest electrical conductivity (of the four metals). **(1)**

(c) It is the hardest **(1)** and its melting point is very high/highest **(1)**.

3 (a) property for 1 mark with relevant reason for 1 mark, e.g. transparent, so you can see through it; tough/strong, so it does not shatter easily.

(b) Glass is brittle/shatters easily **(1)**; the polymer stops pieces of glass hitting the passengers in an accident/the composite material is tougher than glass alone **(1)**.

99. Extended response – Materials

The answer may include some of the following points: **(6)**

FRR:

- cheapest material/about 20 times cheaper than CRP
- about 14 times weaker than CRP
- almost as strong as fibreglass
- slightly stiffer than fibreglass
- about 17 times less stiff than CRP
- low/lowest brittleness
- can be coloured (similar to fibreglass)
- can be pressed into shape/does not have to be built up in layers.

fibreglass:

- twice the cost of FRR
- more than 10 times cheaper than CRP
- about 12 times weaker than CRP
- slightly stronger than FRR
- slightly less stiff than FRR
- 25 times less stiff than CRP
- less brittle than CRP
- more brittle than FRR
- can be coloured (similar to FRR)
- must be built up in layers/cannot be pressed into shape.

CRP:

- most expensive
- expensive/20 times cost of FRR/10 times cost of fibreglass
- strongest material
- about 14 times stronger than FRR
- about 12 times stronger than fibreglass
- stiffest material
- about 17 times stiffer than FRR

- about 25 times stiffer than fibreglass

- most brittle material

- black/cannot be coloured (unlike FRR and fibreglass)

- must be built up in layers/cannot be pressed into shape.

conclusion, for example:

- FRR is best because it is the cheapest, almost as strong as fibreglass, does not shatter easily, can be pressed into shape (similar to steel) and can be coloured so does not need painting.

- Fibreglass is best because it is almost as cheap as FRR and has similar properties, but is stronger than FRR and much less likely to shatter than CRP.

- CRP is best because, although it is much more expensive than the other two materials, it is much stronger so less may need to be used to make the body panels.

Timed Test 1

1 (a) (i) B **(1)**

   (ii) D **(1)**

   (b) 1 mark for each correct value to 4 marks maximum, e.g.

Subatomic particle	Relative mass	Relative charge
proton	1	+1
neutron	1	0
electron	0.0005 or answer in the range 1/1800–1/2000	−1

   (c) They contain 10 protons/the same number of protons **(1)** but neon-20 has 10 neutrons and neon-22 has 12 neutrons/the atoms have different numbers of neutrons **(1)**.

2 (a) D **(1)**

   (b) similarity for 1 mark, e.g. elements in groups/ periods; elements in a group have similar properties

   difference for 1 mark, e.g. Elements in Mendeleev's table are arranged in order of relative atomic mass/elements in modern table arranged in order of atomic number; Mendeleev's table had fewer elements/gaps/ no group 0 elements.

   (c) completed diagram with two crosses on first circle, eight crosses on second circle, five crosses on outer circle for 1 mark:

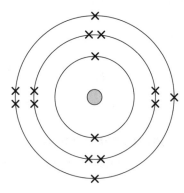

   (d) (i) Atoms of both elements have 1 electron in their outer shell. **(1)**

   Or 2.1 and 2.8.1 with link made to number of electrons in outer shell. **(1)**

   (ii) Atoms of both elements have three occupied shells. **(1)**

   Or 2.8.1 and 2.8.2 with link made to number of occupied shells. **(1)**

3 (a) C **(1)**

   (b) 13 protons **(1)**, 14 neutrons **(1)**, 10 electrons **(1)**

   (c) strong electrostatic forces of attraction/ strong ionic bonds **(1)** between oppositely charged ions **(1)** which need a lot of heat energy to break/overcome **(1)**

   (d) $(35/250) \times 1000$ **(1)**

   $= 140$ g dm^{-3} **(1)**

4 (a) A **(1)**

   (b) dot-and-cross diagram with: one bonding pair of electrons between oxygen and each hydrogen atom **(1)**, two non-bonding pairs of electrons on the oxygen atom **(1)**, e.g.

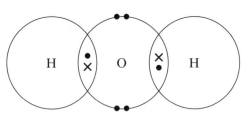

   (c) (i) giant covalent structure/giant covalent lattice **(1)**; many/strong covalent bonds must be broken **(1)** (which needs a lot of energy)

   (ii) Carbon atoms are arranged in layers **(1)** with weak forces between them **(1)**, so the layers easily slide over each other/ graphite is slippery **(1)**.

5 (a) bubbling/fizzing/effervescence **(1)**; magnesium dissolves/disappears **(1)**

   (b) Lighted splint **(1)** ignites gas with a pop **(1)**.

(c) $(9.50 - 2.40) = 7.10$ g **(1)**

(d) division of mass by A_r: Mg $(2.40/24) = 0.1$ *and* Cl $(7.10/35.5) = 0.2$ **(1)**

simplest ratio: 1:2 **(1)**

empirical formula: $MgCl_2$ **(1)**

6 (a) C **(1)**

(b) 1 mark for each correct box, to 4 marks, e.g.

State	Arrangement of particles	Movement of particles
solid	close together regular/ordered	vibrate about fixed positions
liquid	close together random	move around each other
gas	far apart random	rapid in all directions

(c) (i) Particles gain energy/move faster. **(1)**

(ii) A lot of energy/fuel is needed to heat the seawater. **(1)**

(iii) Distilled water does not contain any dissolved salts. **(1)**

(d) (i) removes *solid* particles/insoluble substances **(1)**

(ii) Chlorine is added **(1)** to kill harmful microbes/bacteria (which could cause disease) **(1)**.

7 (a) B **(1)**

(b) Precipitate of iron(III) hydroxide forms. **(1)**

(c) (i) They react with acids to produce a salt and water only. **(1)**

(ii) It is a soluble base/it is a base that dissolves in water. **(1)**

(d) (i) 7 **(1)**

(ii) acidic/acid **(1)**

*(e) *The answer may include some of the following points:* **(6)**

reaction:

- dilute hydrochloric acid/HCl(aq)
- copper oxide/CuO *or* copper carbonate/CuCO$_3$
- word equation: copper oxide + hydrochloric acid → copper chloride + water *or*
- copper carbonate + hydrochloric acid → copper chloride + water + carbon dioxide

- balanced equation: $CuO + 2HCl → CuCl_2 + H_2O$ *or* $CuCO_3 + 2HCl → CuCl_2 + H_2O + CO_2$
- Gently warm the acid.
- Add portions of solid and stir.
- Continue until excess solid is left over.

Preparing the salt:

- Filter to remove the excess solid.
- Heat gently in an evaporating basin/ leave in a warm place
- until crystals form.
- Dry crystals with paper/pour away excess liquid and leave to dry in an oven.

8 (a) ionic compound **(1)** in the molten state/ dissolved in water **(1)**.

(b) B **(1)**

(c) C **(1)**

(d) cathode – zinc **(1)**; anode – chlorine *not chloride* **(1)**

(e) Aluminium is more reactive than carbon. **(1)**

(f) (i) to improve the appearance of a metal object **(1)**; to improve the resistance to corrosion of a metal object **(1)**

(ii) anode – silver *and* cathode – steel cutlery **(1)**; electrolyte: silver nitrate solution **(1)**

9 (a) D **(1)**

(b) (i) $2CuO + C → 2Cu + CO_2$ **(1)**

(ii) $(2.36/2.95) × 100$ **(1)**

$= 80\%$ **(1)**

(iii) two from the following for 1 mark each: the reaction is incomplete; practical losses during the experiment, e.g. pouring/filtering; competing reactions/ unwanted reactions/side reactions

(c) M_r of $SO_2 = 64.0$

total relative mass of all products $= (2 × 63.5) + 64.0 = 191$ **(1)**

atom economy $= 100 × (2 × 63.5)/191$ **(1)**

$= 66.5\%$ **(1)**

10 (a) The reaction is reversible. **(1)**

(b) (i) 450 °C **(1)**

(ii) 200 atmospheres/20 MPa **(1)**

(iii) iron **(1)**

(c) (i) potassium/phosphorus **(1)**

(ii) nitric acid **(1)**

(d) (i) water **(1)**

   (ii) to mix the acid and alkali in the correct proportions/volumes **(1)** needed to obtain a neutral solution/salt solution that does not contain acid or alkali **(1)**

11 (a) One of the reactants is used up. **(1)**

   (b) $2H_2 + O_2 \rightarrow 2H_2O$
   (allow $H_2 + \frac{1}{2}O_2 \rightarrow H_2O$)

   1 mark for correct formulae, 1 mark for balancing

   *(c) *The answer may include some of the following points:* **(6)**

   strengths:

   • quiet

   • emits water vapour only when in use

   • does not take long to refuel/only takes 5 minutes to refuel

   • takes much less time to refuel than a battery-powered forklift takes to recharge

   • medium sized so the forklift truck can move into narrow spaces.

   weaknesses:

   • may be difficult to hear the forklift coming, unlike diesel-powered forklifts

   • water vapour may cause dampness/ condensation unless the warehouse is ventilated

   • takes a little longer to refuel than a diesel-powered forklift

   • larger than a battery-powered forklift so may not fit into all the narrow spaces.

   conclusion in favour of the hydrogen–oxygen fuel cell forklift, e.g. because it can be refuelled quickly (unlike a battery-powered forklift), is quiet and does not release carbon dioxide and smoke (unlike a diesel-powered forklift)

   or

   conclusion against the hydrogen–oxygen fuel cell forklift, e.g. because it is larger than a battery-powered forklift, which is also quiet in use; the battery-powered forklift could be recharged overnight and has no emissions when in use

Timed Test 2

1 (a) A **(1)**

   (b) (i) $2Na(s) + 2H_2O(l) \rightarrow 2NaOH(aq) + H_2(g)$

   1 mark for balancing, 1 mark for state symbols

   (ii) two from the following for 1 mark each: Metal floats; (rapid) fizzing/bubbling; orange/yellow flame; metal disappears; metal moves around.

   (c) (i) 2.8.8.1 **(1)**

   (ii) Sodium atoms are larger than lithium atoms **(1)**; outer electron in sodium is further from the nucleus/more shielded **(1)**; outer electron in sodium is more easily lost/there is a weaker force of attraction between the nucleus and the outer electron **(1)**. *Accept the opposite argument for lithium.*

2 (a) C **(1)**

   (b) *Damp* blue litmus paper **(1)** turns (red then) white/is bleached **(1)**. *or Damp* starch–iodide paper **(1)** turns blue–black **(1)**.

   *(c) *The answer may include some of the following points:* **(6)**

   • A colour change shows that a reaction happens.

   • Bromine reacts with potassium iodide solution.

   • Iodine solution is formed.

   • Colour seen is brown.

   • Bromine displaces iodide ions.

   • bromine + potassium iodide $\rightarrow$ potassium bromide + iodine

   • $Br_2 + 2KI \rightarrow 2KBr + I_2$

   • No visible change shows that no reaction happens.

   • Bromine does not react with potassium chloride solution.

   • Chlorine is more reactive than bromine.

   • Bromine cannot displace chloride ions.

   • Bromine is less reactive than chlorine.

   • Order of reactivity (from most reactive to least reactive halogen) is chlorine, bromine, iodine.

3 (a) D **(1)**

   (b) Limewater **(1)** turns milky/cloudy white **(1)**.

(c) The reaction is exothermic **(1)** because heat energy is given out **(1)**.

(d) (i) Line drawn to the left of the original, starting at origin and with a similar shape **(1)** becomes horizontal at the same volume as the original **(1)**.

  (ii) At a higher concentration the acid particles are more crowded/there are more acid particles in the same volume **(1)**; collisions between particles are more frequent/more collisions per unit time **(1)**.

  (iii) It decreases/it is reduced. **(1)**

4 (a) D **(1)**

(b) minimum energy **(1)** needed for a reaction to start **(1)**

(c) product line (labelled with formulae or as products) to the right and below the reactant line (labelled with formula or as reactant) **(1)**; curve drawn on diagram **(1)**; vertical arrow from height of reactant line to the top of the curve (labelled activation energy) **(1)**. (see part **(d)** (i))

(d) (i) curve drawn below the first and labelled X **(1)**

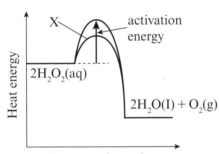

  (ii) speeds up the rate of a reaction **(1)**; is not changed chemically/in mass at the end of the reaction **(1)**

(e) They are biological catalysts. **(1)**

5 (a) B **(1)**

(b) (i) bitumen **(1)**

  (ii) fuel oil **(1)**

  (iii) fuel for aircraft **(1)**

(c) feedstock for the petrochemical industry **(1)**

(d) Crude oil takes millions of years to form/it is being made very slowly/is not being made any more. **(1)**

(e) (i) compounds of hydrogen and carbon **(1)** only **(1)**

  (ii) two from the following, for 1 mark each: number of carbon atoms and

hydrogen atoms in their molecules/size of molecule/relative formula mass; ease of ignition; viscosity

6 (a) D **(1)**

(b) D **(1)**

(c) (i) *Glowing* splint **(1)** relights **(1)**.

  (ii) photosynthesis **(1)** due to the growth of primitive plants **(1)**

(d) (i) Carbon dioxide dissolved in the oceans **(1)** reducing the amount of carbon dioxide in the atmosphere **(1)**.

  (ii) carbon dioxide – burning fossil fuels **(1)**; methane – livestock farming **(1)**

  (iii) one from the following, for 1 mark: climate change/rising sea levels/melting ice caps/change in distribution of animals or plants

7 (a) C **(1)**

(b) (i) sulfur **(1)**

  (ii) two from the following, for 1 mark each: damages statues/buildings/stonework/limestone; damages iron/steel; damages trees/plants; harms aquatic organisms, e.g. fish

(c) (i) $N_2(g) + 2O_2(g) \rightarrow 2NO_2(g)$

  Or $\frac{1}{2}N_2(g) + O_2(g) \rightarrow NO_2(g)$

  1 mark for formulae, 1 mark for balancing, 1 mark for state symbols

  (ii) the air **(1)**

  (iii) hot/high temperature **(1)**

(d) It combines with haemoglobin/red blood cells **(1)** which reduces the amount of oxygen that can be carried by the blood **(1)**.

8 (a) B **(1)**

(b) C **(1)**

(c) compound **A** – sodium **(1)** carbonate **(1)**; compound **B** – lithium **(1)** sulfate **(1)**

*(d) *The answer may include some of the following points:* **(6)**

  • Dissolve powders in water.

  • Add the solutions to test tubes.

  • Add a few drops of dilute sodium hydroxide solution.

  • Shake to mix.

  • Observe the colour of any precipitates formed.

  • Iron(II)/Fe^{2+}/iron(II) chloride gives a pale-green precipitate.

- Pale-green precipitate gradually turns orange–brown on standing.
- Aluminium/Al^{3+}/aluminium chloride gives a white precipitate.
- White precipitate redissolves/ disappears when excess sodium hydroxide solution is added.
- Calcium/Ca^{2+}/calcium chloride gives a white precipitate.
- White precipitate does not redissolve/ disappear when excess sodium hydroxide solution is added.

9 (a) B **(1)**

   (b) (i) C_4H_8 **(1)**

      (ii) Drawn structure of but-2-ene (2), e.g.

$$H-\underset{\underset{H}{|}}{\overset{\overset{H}{|}}{C}}-\underset{\underset{H}{|}}{\overset{\overset{H}{|}}{C}}=\underset{}{\overset{\overset{H}{|}}{C}}-\underset{\underset{H}{|}}{\overset{\overset{H}{|}}{C}}-H$$

H atoms on the C=C atoms can be both up, both down or one up one down.

If atoms and bonds are correct, but C=C is in the wrong place, 1 mark only.

   (c) (i) It contains a C=C bond/carbon–carbon double bond. **(1)**

      (ii) Add bromine water to each substance: changes from orange–brown to colourless with ethene **(1)**; no change/ stays orange–brown with ethane **(1)**

If orange–brown not mentioned, 1 mark maximum.

(d) A **(1)**

10 (a) D **(1)**

   (b) A substance of high average relative molecular mass **(1)** made up of small repeating units **(1)**.

   (c) (i) poly(propene) **(1)**

      (ii) structure of repeating unit of poly(propene), e.g.

1 mark for correct positions of atoms and CH_3 group; 1 mark for C–C bond and brackets (with or without *n* outside)

      (iii) carbon dioxide **(1)** water **(1)**

(d) situation **(1)** with problem it causes **(1)**, e.g. Polymers are non-biodegradable so they take a long time to rot/decompose/they fill up landfill sites; some cannot be recycled so they waste finite resources/crude oil; they produce gases when burnt, which may be harmful/toxic/ contribute to global warming; waste polymers need to be sorted so they can be recycled, which is expensive/time-consuming/difficult to do.

The Periodic Table of the Elements

Key

| relative atomic mass |
| **atomic symbol** |
| name |
| atomic (proton) number |

																	4 **He** helium 2

1	**2**											**3**	**4**	**5**	**6**	**7**	**0**
						1 **H** hydrogen 1											4 **He** helium 2
7 **Li** lithium 3	9 **Be** beryllium 4											11 **B** boron 5	12 **C** carbon 6	14 **N** nitrogen 7	16 **O** oxygen 8	19 **F** fluorine 9	20 **Ne** neon 10
23 **Na** sodium 11	24 **Mg** magnesium 12											27 **Al** aluminium 13	28 **Si** silicon 14	31 **P** phosphorus 15	32 **S** sulfur 16	35.5 **Cl** chlorine 17	40 **Ar** argon 18
39 **K** potassium 19	40 **Ca** calcium 20	45 **Sc** scandium 21	48 **Ti** titanium 22	51 **V** vanadium 23	52 **Cr** chromium 24	55 **Mn** manganese 25	56 **Fe** iron 26	59 **Co** cobalt 27	59 **Ni** nickel 28	63.5 **Cu** copper 29	65 **Zn** zinc 30	70 **Ga** gallium 31	73 **Ge** germanium 32	75 **As** arsenic 33	79 **Se** selenium 34	80 **Br** bromine 35	84 **Kr** krypton 36
85 **Rb** rubidium 37	88 **Sr** strontium 38	89 **Y** yttrium 39	91 **Zr** zirconium 40	93 **Nb** niobium 41	96 **Mo** molybdenum 42	[98] **Tc** technetium 43	101 **Ru** ruthenium 44	103 **Rh** rhodium 45	106 **Pd** palladium 46	108 **Ag** silver 47	112 **Cd** cadmium 49	115 **In** indium 49	119 **Sn** tin 50	122 **Sb** antimony 51	128 **Te** tellurium 52	127 **I** iodine 53	131 **Xe** xenon 54
133 **Cs** caesium 55	137 **Ba** barium 56	139 **La*** lanthanum 57	178 **Hf** hafnium 72	181 **Ta** tantalum 73	184 **W** tungsten 74	186 **Re** rhenium 75	190 **Os** osmium 76	192 **Ir** iridium 77	195 **Pt** platinum 78	197 **Au** gold 79	201 **Hg** mercury 80	204 **Tl** thallium 81	207 **Pb** lead 82	209 **Bi** bismuth 83	[209] **Po** polonium 84	[210] **At** astatine 85	[222] **Rn** radon 86
[223] **Fr** francium 87	[226] **Ra** radium 88	[227] **Ac*** actinium 89	[261] **Rf** rutherfordium 104	[262] **Db** dubnium 105	[266] **Sg** seaborgium 106	[264] **Bh** bohrium 107	[277] **Hs** hassium 108	[268] **Mt** meitnerium 109	[271] **Ds** darmstadtium 110	[272] **Rg** roentgenium 111							

Elements with atomic numbers 112–116 have been reported but not fully authenticated

*The lanthanoids (atomic numbers 58–71) and the actinoids (atomic numbers 90–103) have been omitted.

The relative atomic masses of copper and chlorine have been rounded to the nearest whole number.

Published by Pearson Education Limited, 80 Strand, London, WC2R 0RL.

www.pearsonschoolsandfecolleges.co.uk

Copies of official specifications for all Edexcel qualifications may be found on the website: www.edexcel.com

Text and illustrations © Pearson Education Limited 2017
Typeset, illustrated and produced by Phoenix Photosetting
Cover illustration by Miriam Sturdee

The right of Nigel Saunders to be identified as author of this work has been asserted by him in accordance with the Copyright, Designs and Patents Act 1988.

First published 2017

20 19 18 17
10 9 8 7 6 5 4 3 2 1

British Library Cataloguing in Publication Data
A catalogue record for this book is available from the British Library

ISBN 978 1 292 13193 1

Printed in Slovakia by Neografia

Acknowledgements
The author and publisher would like to thank Roderick Stinton and Noyan Erdenizci for their contribution. Content written by Ian Roberts and Damian Riddle is included.
The author and publisher would like to thank the following individuals and organisations for permission to reproduce photographs:

Alamy Images: Bruce Boulton.co.uk 79; **Pearson Education Ltd:** Trevor Clifford 96

All other images © Pearson Education

Some content has been reused from the following titles:
9781292131948 Revise Edexcel GCSE Chemistry Higher Tier Revision Workbook (2016) by Nigel Saunders;
9781446902622 Revise Edexcel GCSE Science Revision Workbook Higher by Peter Ellis, Damian Riddle,
Ian Roberts, Julia Salter
9781446902660 Revise Edexcel GCSE Additional Science Revision Workbook Higher by Peter Ellis,
Damian Riddle, Ian Roberts
9781446902585 Revise Edexcel GCSE Science Extension Units Revision Workbook by Peter Ellis, Damian Riddle,
Stephen Winrow-Campbell

A note from the publisher
In order to ensure that this resource offers high-quality support for the associated Pearson qualification, it has been through a review process by the awarding body. This process confirms that this resource fully covers the teaching and learning content of the specification or part of a specification at which it is aimed. It also confirms that it demonstrates an appropriate balance between the development of subject skills, knowledge and understanding, in addition to preparation for assessment.

Endorsement does not cover any guidance on assessment activities or processes (e.g. practice questions or advice on how to answer assessment questions), included in the resource nor does it prescribe any particular approach to the teaching or delivery of a related course.

While the publishers have made every attempt to ensure that advice on the qualification and its assessment is accurate, the official specification and associated assessment guidance materials are the only authoritative source of information and should always be referred to for definitive guidance.

Examiners will not use endorsed resources as a source of material for any assessment set by Pearson.

Endorsement of a resource does not mean that the resource is required to achieve this Pearson qualification, nor does it mean that it is the only suitable material available to support the qualification, and any resource lists produced by the awarding body shall include this and other appropriate resources.